CW01023892

# In Conversation with Bessie Head

# In Conversation with Bessie Head

Mary S. Lederer

BLOOMSBURY ACADEMIC
NEW YORK • LONDON • OXFORD • NEW DELHI • SYDNEY

BLOOMSBURY ACADEMIC
Bloomsbury Publishing Inc
1385 Broadway, New York, NY 10018, USA
50 Bedford Square, London, WC1B 3DP, UK

BLOOMSBURY, BLOOMSBURY ACADEMIC and the Diana logo are trademarks of
Bloomsbury Publishing Plc

First published in the United States of America 2019

Cover design: Eleanor Rose
Cover images: Portrait © E. and M. Kgosi, courtesy of Khama III Memorial Museum,
Serowe, Botswana; Postcard frame © Getty Images

A catalog record for this book is available from the Library of Congress.

ISBN: HB: 978-1-5013-5140-2
ePDF: 978-1-5013-5142-6
eBook: 978-1-5013-5141-9

Typeset by Newgen KnowledgeWorks Pvt. Ltd., Chennai, India

To find out more about our authors and books visit www.bloomsbury.com
and sign up for our newsletters.

*To my nieces and nephew*
*Jennifer Kate Lederer,*
*Rachel Anne Lederer,*
*Elizabeth Helen Wallis,*
*Angus John Wallis,*
*Clara Marie Lederer,*
*and*
*Hiba Mary Ann Lederer;*
*to my father*
*James David Lederer;*
*and to the memory of my mother*
*Mary Ann Lederer.*

# Contents

# Acknowledgments

An undertaking such as this requires more people than can be named to keep the writer going. I would like to draw attention to the following people in particular.

For academic assistance, I would like to thank Donald Cosentino, Kathleen Komar, the late Mazisi Kunene, the late Beverly Robinson, and William Worger. My friends Sandra Banks, Wendy Belcher, Angela Lee, Marilyn Manners, Jeff Miller, Eva Navarro, and the late Jessica Werner offered emotional and social support. My sister Anne Lederer gave me a desperately needed month at her apartment in Paris and always helped put things in perspective.

Michelle Commeyras, the late Janet Hermans, Tom Holzinger, Anne Lederer, Katy Lederer, Grant Lilford, Reshoketjoe Lilford, and Leloba Molema all read and gave valuable comments. My late uncle Richard Lederer (not the other Richard Lederer, but my Uncle Dick), my friend Wendy Belcher, my cousin Mark Lederer, and my father-in-law Bob Bennett all responded cheerfully to endless requests to send material that I would not otherwise have had access to. Harold Head, Ed Wilson, and the Bessie Head Estate gave generous permission to quote extensively from Bessie Head's papers. Gasenone Kediseng of the Khama III Memorial Museum in Serowe graciously responded to panicked phone calls regarding yet another letter I needed to look at. Gase is a marvel of helpfulness, and her knowledge of the Bessie Head Papers merits special note.

Tom Holzinger, Linda-Susan Beard, and Sue Houchins are fellow Bessie-philes, and we conduct ongoing conversations about many things Bessie. In March 2011, I presented preliminary ideas for this book to a seminar for the English Department at the University of Botswana, and I am grateful for the helpful and insightful comments from those present. From January to May 2011, I co-taught, with Seatholo Tumedi, the fourth-year Bessie Head course at the University of Botswana. I enjoyed the discussions with students and with Seatholo, and I thank them also for their insights.

One spring morning on one of our regular walks, when I was struggling with how to approach the "question" of women in the novels, Leloba Molema brought up the concept of responsibility. Kirsten Hill once remarked on the paradox of the "gesture of belonging," a comment that haunted me for many years. I thank them both for cutting through to the essential point.

Margaret Daymond, fellow Bessie scholar in Durban, read the manuscript and made many suggestions that helped clarify some of the awkward spots. Many, many thanks, Margaret.

Many thanks also to the reviewers of this manuscript, for also helping me see the solution to a particular problem.

I am undoubtedly forgetting many people who have talked with me about the issues that have arisen for me through various readings of Bessie Head, and for leaving out those names, I beg forgiveness. My memory just isn't what it used to be.

I must not, of course, forget my family, who remind me constantly of what is most important.

Finally, I again thank my husband Bruce Bennett, my most enthusiastic publicist and the best reader of everything I write. We met halfway through my life, but I cannot imagine going the rest of the way without him.

# 1

# Reading Bessie Head

*I have only two themes . . . that love is really good . . . and . . . that it is*
*important to be an ordinary person.*

Betty Fradkin, "Conversations with Bessie" 433

The face of Zoë Wicomb gazed mutely at me.[1] I was standing in the book center in Maseru, Lesotho, in early 1987. Her photograph took up the whole cover of *Maru*, by Bessie Head. I'd never read an African novel before, having just completed a master's degree in German. I was a Peace Corps volunteer, teaching high-school mathematics at a Catholic girls' school, and I was looking for something "relevant" to read.

Since I had done German women's writing for my master's, I was looking for an African woman writer, preferably Southern African. Head's novel was the only one on the shelf, and it was short (and therefore relatively inexpensive, an important consideration for a Peace Corps volunteer). So I bought it, took it with me back to my village home, and read it. Two years later I started an MA and then a PhD program in African literature, in order to study Bessie Head. Who was this woman who changed the course of my intellectual and spiritual life?

In 1964, Bessie Head accepted permanent exile from South Africa to take a teaching post in Botswana, where she lived until her death in 1986. In his introduction to *A Gesture of Belonging*, Randolph Vigne wrote about her,

> The product of a deeply disturbing, insecure childhood, tortured by her status as a "Coloured" (while belonging to no community designated by that

---

1 Zoë Wicomb is an important contemporary South African writer, but she had not been published when George Hallett took the photograph on the cover of *Maru*.

term in the evil system of apartheid), constantly brooding on the story of her mother's mental illness and her own conception, she was haunted by an abiding sense of alienation and aloneness, the fear of madness and the sense of a coming early death. (6)

For someone with this sort of background to write that "love is really good" takes an enormous strength of will, a will that jumped out from the pages of *Maru*. For Bessie Head the writer, love was an important concept, but for Bessie Head the human being, it must also have seemed very elusive. I was only just beginning to learn not to scoff at love, so *Maru*, though a hard read, was a gripping one. Bessie's will pulled me into the pages, and I wanted more.

Two days after I turned in my PhD dissertation, I received a copy of Bessie Head's biography, Gillian Stead Eilersen's *Bessie Head: Thunder behind Her Ears. Her Life and Writing*, that a friend had been able to find in South Africa. It is very thorough and well documented. Her life story was intriguing and also—for someone like me—depressing. For all that my parents (predictably) drove me crazy,[2] they were a huge, important, and supportive part of my life. What would I have done if, like Bessie, I had been so alone?

The short version of Head's life can be given fairly quickly: she was born in 1937 in a psychiatric hospital in Pietermaritzburg to a white mother; her father was unknown.[3] She was returned by the first foster family she was placed with because she was developing black physical characteristics. She was then placed with a "Coloured"[4] family in Pietermaritzburg and raised by them until she was placed in a mission boarding school, where she discovered her true origins. She worked as a journalist for a period, married and had a son, dabbled in politics, and then, as her marriage failed and she became disillusioned with opposition politics, moved to permanent exile in Botswana, where she worked as a teacher, typist, and gardener—and writer—to support herself and her son. She died in Serowe in 1986.

---

2  I was still pretty stupid at that point.
3  See Tom Holzinger, "The Black Antecedents of Bessie Amelia Emery Head," for some discussion and speculation on the possible identity of Head's father.
4  "Coloured" in South Africa refers to a sort of ethnic group: its members are descended from the white and Khoi and Cape Malay intermarriages of the seventeenth and eighteenth centuries. Bessie Head was only technically a member since she was not descended from them but born of an illegal sexual union.

Head herself told the following story in her introduction to the story "Witchcraft," published in *Ms.* magazine in November 1975:

> I was born on the sixth of July, 1937, in the Pietermaritzburg Mental Hospital . . . The reason for my peculiar birthplace was that my mother was white, and she had acquired me from a black man. She was judged insane, and committed to the mental hospital while pregnant. Her name was Bessie Emery and I consider it the only honor South Africans ever did me—naming me after this unknown, lovely, and unpredictable woman. (72)

In the years since Head's death, much more information about her life has come to light, and more critical attention devoted to examining how Head created a life story that suited her needs, looking in particular at the relationship between her life, her published work, and her letters.[5] Although Head herself certainly knew the bare facts—about her place of birth and the circumstances of her upbringing—she only knew a fraction of what we now know. At the time of her death, she had been contracted to write an autobiography, but she became ill and died before she could begin working on it.

About a year after I got my degree, a lecturer position opened up at the University of Botswana. I applied, was hired, and arrived in Gaborone in September 1997. I was here. Only 400 kilometers from Bessie Head's home in Serowe. In the twenty years that I have lived here, I have been carrying on a conversation—a back-and-forth relationship of sorts—with Bessie, with colleagues, with family and friends, with critics, about her writing, about Botswana, about myself. Of course I didn't realize it then, but the conversation really began when I started thinking about prophecy and deity during the work on my dissertation. I didn't want to believe in God (I had, about five years earlier, confidently declared myself a Marxist atheist), but I think I wanted to believe in something. Bessie showed me that my lack of belief was based largely on ignorance. And that I had to sort that problem out for myself. Reading her, reading about her life, and thinking about my life seems a good place to start.

---

5 See, e.g., the following in *The Life and Work of Bessie Head*: Linda-Susan Beard, "Letter by Letter: Bessie Head's Epistolary Art"; Gwendolyn Etter-Lewis, " 'Raising Hell': The Body as Text in Selected Letters of Bessie Head"; and Sisi Maqagi, "Epistolary Transgressions." See also Annie Gagiano, "Writing a Life in Epistolic Form: Bessie Head's Letters."

Bessie Head drew very heavily on her own life for material to write about. Her own narration of the story of her life resembles the details she gave to her character Elizabeth in *A Question of Power*: daughter of a white woman, born in a psychiatric hospital, shunned by her mother's family and shunted around and ostracized because of her background, finally landing in Botswana with a young son, and experiencing episodes of mental breakdown. What *A Question of Power* represents, however, is less a representation of Head's life—although it is certainly autobiographical—than a fictionalization of her life placed in the context of a worldview she began to develop very early in her writing, including in her voluminous correspondence.[6] Some of her earliest short pieces raise questions that would, nearly twenty years later, become cornerstones of her philosophy; the imagery of the following passage, for example, suggests seven heavenly virtues, seven deadly sins, the honesty that she would strive for in her relationships with others, the unity of souls, the omnipresence of God, the nature of love, and contradiction:

> All my seven faces of deceit and pretence I had put down. Only my nameless face was there because the earth was breathing, and the air was still and quiet. Then I was trapped too, like the rain clouds. I had no time to find my seven faces, for you came to me silently, and when I looked up you were there; also with your nameless face . . . A thousand differing contradictions pour out to conceal the underground stream that is the same always, flowing, continuous. Now I am plunged in head-to-toe; amazed that my whole self flows outward into you, yet back to me again in a current of deep peace without beginning or ending. ("Earth and Everything" 139–40)

Her philosophy covers love, community, faith, and the nature of good and evil in the human being. This book will trace the development of that philosophy in her writing from *When Rain Clouds Gather* through *Maru* to *A Question of Power*, in the context of much of her other writing, but because Bessie Head draws her readers into that context, and because we draw on our own

---

6  Already in 1960, she wrote to Langston Hughes, "I would wish you a merry xmas but I am not a Christian! But still. I love all things in this world. Good like the 'virgin' birth of Christ. And bad. Like Christianity" ("The Bessie Head—Langston Hughes Correspondence, 1960–61" 13).

lives when we read her, this discussion will also offer a somewhat personal perspective—mine.[7]

\* \* \*

> [R]eading can also be a form of dialogue which does not simply validate stereotypes, rigid preconceptions or brittle political and academic theories through texts, but truly recognizes writing as a communicative act. The ideal of reciprocal dialogues was central for Bessie Head, and they functioned in her fiction as a trope for all liberating relationships. Her prolific letter-writing also revealed a passionate belief about communicating through writing, especially communicating across boundaries, and with an ardent faith in the human need to share ideals, pleasures and challenges, while also acknowledging the "strangeness" of others' views. ("Bessie Head's Freedoms")

I begin with this quotation from Desiree Lewis because it captures an essential aspect of the experience of reading Bessie Head: what matters is not only what the books are about, and not only the experience we bring to them, but also what we experience from reading them. This is the communication between reader and writer that Head desires. The tone of her letters seemed to beg for replies, and the letters themselves placed her in a network of communication with people who, in many cases, did not even know each other and some of whom she herself had never met but who had read her books and reached out to her to continue their discussions about her work. Charlotte Bruner wrote to Head that "[y]our letters are generous and reveal things to me about myself as well" (KMM 40 BHP 12,[8] August 23, 1978). This kind of reading is not easy, nor is it really "over" when one of Head's novels ends. She grabs her readers by the lapels and hauls them into her work,[9] and to finish reading it does not often give a sense of satisfaction.

Head's own needs regarding her life story would have been those of a story-teller as well as philosopher. Much of her material does come from her

---

7 I am following the publication order of the books, although I first read them in a different order (*Maru, A Question of Power, When Rain Clouds Gather*), and in fact I think the order matters less than the content.

8 All quotations from the Bessie Head Papers (held at the Khama III Memorial Museum in Serowe, Botswana) will be cited in the text by their file and document numbers.

9 Or, as Jacqueline Rose wrote, "I am sure I am not the only reader to have experienced *A Question of Power* as writing by battery assault" (404).

own life in Serowe. Reading her unpublished letters reveals even more clearly the link between what she published and what she wrote to others.[10] About a forthcoming collection, Linda-Susan Beard writes that Head's "hybridized experiments in narrative have counterparts and first drafts in one of the largest collections of extant African epistles . . . Bessie [destroyed] almost one thousand letters shortly before her death because of the limitations of space in her tiny Serowe home. Putting aside the poignancy of loss, what we have is a final collection that represents Bessie's own editorial logic" ("Letter by Letter: Bessie Head's Epistolary Art" 201). She was someone who loved language: formulations, phrases, words are repeated in letters to different people, almost as if she were testing variations on different people to find out how they sounded, both to herself and to others. In a 1961 letter to Cordelia Guenther, her flat mate in Cape Town, she writes that she will be working late at the library: "This poem is most difficult. I have started and destroyed it again and again" (Bessie Head to Cordelia Guenther, undated, uncatalogued KMM BHP). The "poem" is the lyrics to "Black Coffee"; she must have listened to it over and over in order to get it right. The letter includes her attempt to record the words of the song (and some of them are incorrect). This is the first known illustration of a habit she often followed: handwriting the words of a passage, poem, or song in order to really understand the craft and meaning. In her own writing, she valued feedback, and her correspondence is also an important component in her project of bringing people and readers into conversation with her.

When Head herself was ready to write, she typed out one original and two carbons. She did not, with the exception of the final chapters of *When Rain Clouds Gather*, rework her material very much. Once the manuscript was done, it was done. She would have had to make any corrections on the original and both carbons, or else type the whole thing over again, an onerous task in pre-word-processing days. She worked in her garden full-time during the day and did most of her writing at night by candlelight.

---

10 "Most of Head's letters are humorous, thoughtfully-written and extremely readable. But the way they register her distinctive fictional practices makes them integral to an understanding of her epistemology and narrative practices" (Lewis, *Living on a Horizon* 44).

\* \* \*

Head's own experiences and those she wrote demonstrate a thorough and personal understanding of the nature of oppression and its human consequences. Her construction of her characters' experiences and her formulation of positive human communities reflects an awareness of social forces and how they act on individuals. Her comments to Vigne, in a letter of September 24, 1981, regarding public response to her illness also suggest that what she wrote about struck a public chord: "Surprisingly, a number of people pulled out breakdowns in sympathy . . . Nearly every house I walked into had a nervous breakdown in it, mostly women and some astonishing confessions: 'I've been married twice and I'm not happy. Marital problems gave me a breakdown last year.' Some people simply cooked up nervous troubles as far as I could see!" (*A Gesture of Belonging* 153). Such public reaction undoubtedly pleased her, but her comments also point to an ability to observe and portray human behavior in a way that makes personal trauma familiar. Head wrote about both personal trauma and social discomfort, about pain and oppression, but also—and for Head these two were clearly related—about remaking God and reshaping the world to be fit for human beings.

Head's own thinking about the nature of God and the problems of human society and human existence stretched over many broad, different traditions. She was brought up in a Catholic environment (*Thunder behind Her Ears* 17–25) and attended school at an Anglican mission.[11] She read widely in the M. L. Sultan Indian library in Durban,[12] where she encountered texts in the Hindu tradition. It is clear from her writing that she was familiar with the Bible, but she was also familiar with important religious texts from Hindu and Buddhist traditions. *A Question of Power* in particular incorporates all these, as well as elements of Greek mythology and the famous reference to Islam,

---

11 Eilersen suggests that being forcibly separated from her foster mother and made to abandon her Roman Catholic faith, along with her negative experiences at the Anglican school at St. Monica's, engendered a hatred for Christianity, but that she nevertheless retained some regard for Roman Catholicism. She did ask Howard to contact a Roman Catholic priest when she died (*Thunder behind Her Ears* 25–26).

12 "This was a library that had been donated to the Indians of the city by one of their own wealthy merchants but was open to anyone interested in reading. [Bessie Head] joined it" (*Thunder behind Her Ears* 34–35).

"There is only one God, and his name is Man. And Elizabeth is his prophet" (*A Question of Power* 206).[13]

The broadness of her approach and the skill of her writing mean that many "readings" of Head are possible. These frameworks can provide a place to start, a point of contact between reader and writer, but they are also somewhat unsatisfactory, in part because in order to make sense, they have to overlook the contradictions in the texts themselves. Most commonly, her writing is embraced by postcolonial critics, and *A Question of Power* turns up on any number of world and postcolonial literature syllabi. Certainly her work addresses colonial and patriarchal power relationships and exposes the social causes that create madness[14] in women and others. But her writing is not postcolonial or feminist in any easily categorizable way. She herself adamantly objected to any label at all, steadfastly asserting, her whole life, that "political camps falsify truth" ("Some Notes on Novel Writing" 63), and by "political camps" she meant any ideology whatsoever.[15] For Bessie Head, the role of individual responsibility was too important and too significant to let anyone off the hook—she noted that "I could be evil, too" ("Some Notes on Novel Writing" 63)—and she rejected all forms of power, including postcolonial, postindependence, nationalist, and neocolonial ones.

Human companionship has a much more ambiguous position in her writing: it is desired in all three novels, but it is nevertheless the source of much agony. Head's writing in particular lays bare that agony and then reconstitutes the human relationships, always reimagining them in utopian ways but also always from the perspective of a character who remains a bit outside of those same relationships. For example, the famous "gesture of belonging" at the end of *A Question of Power* (206) occurs when Elizabeth is alone in her room.

---

13  See June M. Campbell, "Beyond Duality: A Buddhist Reading of Bessie Head's *A Question of Power*," for a Buddhist reading, and Bruce S. Bennett, "Ecumenical Readings of Bessie Head," for a more general overview of the possibilities for reading Head in a religious context.

14  I will use the term *madness* in a very loose sense, not to refer necessarily to insanity or clinical illness, but to refer to a general characterization of Elizabeth's experiences.

15  In "My Home," Head writes of the emotional content of her "home" and concludes, "Tread softly— the walls breath[e] peace. Deep, dark, black peace, and the wind don't blow" (145). The phrase "and the wind don't blow" is repeated in every paragraph and probably has several references: in 1960 in Cape Town, Harold Macmillan made his famous "winds of change" speech; one of Head's poems from the period takes the same title; she was also working on a novel at the time and gave the title to the manuscript (now probably lost).

Head's novels examine the social relationships that shape our individual behavior, and they also reflect her own attempts to understand the situation of individuals where they live, and not just in conflict with their communities. Her writing reflects an understanding of the way people are constituted as whole beings: we are unique but at the same time we depend on others to confirm our uniqueness, our identity. This is the difficulty of reading Bessie Head as well as of just being human, and it requires creating a dialogue with other readings, other literature, and other readers.

This book will attempt to trace, explore, and open up the experience—my experience—of reading and of understanding Head's work by addressing the totality of her thought[16] as she expressed it in her major trilogy (*When Rain Clouds Gather, Maru*, and *A Question of Power*)[17] and as she developed the philosophy of "the brotherhood of man" (*A Question of Power* 206) and of God. The novels explore questions regarding the social, psychological, and spiritual nature of human beings, but they also explore the gaps that each way of explaining and knowing human behavior leaves open. By the time the vision is most fully articulated, in *A Question of Power*, Elizabeth is able to embrace the contradictions in herself and in society. Issues of race and gender determine the character of Elizabeth's madness and salvation, and the paradoxical relationship between individual and community exposes the tensions that exacerbate her situation but also enable Elizabeth to realize her potential. The spiritual dimension of experience—what some call the exploration of the soul—ultimately makes it possible for Elizabeth to successfully integrate her experiences into the way she defines her place in society. I will also refer to Head's other writings as a way of engaging in a kind of dialogue with her, and I will make a few comparisons with other texts, especially *The Grass Is Singing* by Doris Lessing, which I first read at the same time that I first read *A*

---

16 If my discussion is successful, however, then the totality will be amorphous and blurry.

17 Arthur Ravenscroft wrote that "I do see these three novels as very closely related to one another, and the third in many ways helps to explicate the first and second" (175). Eilersen also wrote of them as a trilogy: "Bessie is acknowledging the process of examining or reworking her own experiences in her three novels which has been progressively intensified. Seen together they constitute a trilogy; an untraditional trilogy in that the movement is inward rather than forward" (*Thunder behind Her Ears* 176). Bessie Head herself wrote, "All three books are concerned with stating a personal choice and an anxiety that that personal choice be the right one" (KMM 152 BHP 4, June 26, 1980, to Charles Sarvan).

*Question of Power* (so I have thought for a long time about the similarities and differences between them).

* * *

The original form of this book, in order to be a "proper" dissertation, offered some kind of literary analysis based on certain theoretical constructs (as a literature dissertation is supposed to do). But over the course of the more than twenty years since I completed it, I have evolved into someone else, and so this book must be different; it must be more. The dissertation is no longer adequate or even, in many ways, correct. This book represents a change in my way of looking at the world and a fundamental shift in how I perceive the profession I trained for.

I was twenty-three when I discovered metaphor. I was in a third-year introductory German literature class. We had been assigned Hugo von Hofmannsthal's "*Weltgeheimnis*" and Stefan Georg's "*Das Wort*." I knew what a metaphor was, of course, but these two poems were a revelation: they are about language, discourses on the nature of what words could *mean*, in the most complex sense. I copied the poems over and over in my diary, and memorized them and recited them repeatedly to myself.

As we (my classmates and I) progressed, though, and were introduced to theory, I began to flounder. In the first place, the theoretical material that we read was so dry and uninteresting that I had a hard time simply reading it, in complete contrast to those poems and other literature that engaged me for hours at a stretch. I didn't copy passages from theory in my diary. I learned about reader-response theory, structuralism, deconstruction; psychological, Marxist, feminist, modernist approaches; New Criticism. All that.

Looking back, I think now that I was disturbed by the way all these approaches seemed to coldly categorize my responses to something that moved me so much. I think I understood the process of using theory to analyze a text, but I couldn't see the point of it. Still, I kept at it, reading the literature I enjoyed and performing the analyses that were expected of me. I got a BA, then an MA, then went to Lesotho and bumped into Bessie in the bookshop, then did another MA and a PhD, and started, as it were, the rest of my intellectual and academic life.

I am still fascinated by metaphor, and I can still recite "*Weltgeheimnis*" and "*Das Wort*" from memory (if a bit haltingly; after all, it has been more than thirty years since I first learned them). How can a word "mean" two different things, at the same time? But while I am interested in some theoretical issues, I have a fairly strong aversion to theory itself.[18]

At the end of the first chapter of *A Very Short Introduction to Literary Theory*, Jonathan Culler makes some assertions about theory that relate to the ideas that I am exploring in this book. Here are his remarks:

> Theory makes you desire mastery: you hope that theoretical reading will give you the concepts to organize and understand the phenomena that concern you. But theory makes mastery impossible, not only because there is always more to know, but, more specifically and more painfully, because theory is itself the questioning of presumed results and the assumptions on which they are based . . . You have not become master, but neither are you where you were before. You reflect on your reading in new ways. You have different questions to ask and a better sense of the implications of the questions you put to works you read. (16)

I am attracted to the uncertainty that Culler describes in the above paragraph, and I understand the drive to try and "organize." It is part of human nature to try to make sense of our surroundings by organizing the way we understand them. This drive has been part of human life since, as my former students liked to say, time immemorial, or at least since the time of Plato, whose work is often the start point for introductory courses on theory.

But instead of organizing our impressions, I believe that Bessie Head's writing fosters uncertainty, and not about any preconceived ideas about structures, and certainly not only about the questions we put to what we read. First of all, I think that Head would say that all structures are simply about power, and we have to find ways to eliminate the effects of power on human life. And second, we must do this by examining ourselves and our own lives, not only or even primarily by examining the institutions that govern our lives. We must examine our own relationship to power in order to understand how

---

18 I am not the only person to feel this way, of course. See, for one example, Barbara Christian, "The Race for Theory," and the final chapter of this book.

to eliminate it, even though total elimination might not be possible. We can do this through reading. What Culler says about theory and mastery is absolutely true, at least for me: when I finish reading Bessie Head, I have not become master of the texts, even though I desire to, but I have learned something about myself.

If what I propose is organized, in any way, I suppose it puts me on the threshold of a new way of thinking about reading that could be considered— oh, horror!—theoretical. But it is theory individually determined, a kind of "idio-theory" of reading. Our responses to what we read are guided by all sorts of things, including, but not exclusively, the theories and methodology and methods that we know. They are guided also by our lives, our relationships, our previous readings of the same material and of other material, including, I think, books that we read as children, as well as books that were read to us. They are guided by what kinds of books we like, what kind of music we listen to, where we live, and how we react emotionally, viscerally, to the things that happen to us. Because this constellation of "things" is probably unique to each individual, the "theory" with which we approach reading in this—my?— model is not really theoretical in any useful way, in that it cannot be applied to any other reader.

Why? Because I don't want to generalize. I want to personalize. My aversion to theory represents an aversion to that generalizing, even homogenizing, impulse that destroys the excitement of reading something extraordinary. I am much more interested in how I am affected by literature, and in the case of Bessie Head's work, I am interested in how I have been affected over a long period of time. I find that my responses cannot be contained within theoretical categories, and neither can Bessie Head's writing. If my responses were that cold, that impartial, then I would have failed, and I would have failed Bessie Head.

Reader-response criticism, I think, contains that same generalizing impulse. Reader-response criticism maintains that the understanding of a text changes according to what experiences and attitudes a given reader brings to it. There are even new approaches that measure responses to literature using psychological models, but again, suggesting something about the experience that is generalizable, overlooking the alchemy of an eager reader encountering a work of literature (or any work of art) that touches the heart and soul and life in an inexplicable, undefinable way. Once a reader responds, in that model, the response becomes codified. What I propose takes the perhaps obvious premise that reading a text changes the reader, but more particularly, I think that Bessie Head's texts change the same reader with each reading; thus reading a Bessie Head text becomes an ongoing and ever-evolving conversation. In this kind of reading, author intent is not irrelevant, as it is for reader response and most other types of criticism and theory, but rather it forms a part of all the experiences that a reader brings to the work *and* that the writer brings to the work, and so it becomes part of the conversation.

As I groped around in the early stages of reworking my dissertation into this book, still feeling like I needed to tie my ideas onto some theoretical or anti-theoretical post, I stumbled into personal criticism. This field contains some interesting ideas, which I will consider next, but most importantly it gave me some courage and the sense that I might not be alone in my desire to recapture the joy of reading and the sense of engaging with another human being's mind, which led me to literature in the first place. Conventional literary theory, in its totalizing attempts to explain ideology by avoiding bias, in fact gets in the way of that joy and engagement by placing itself between the person who wrote and the one who reads the text.

In order to understand personal criticism, I went back to two important essays from 1987 and 1989, in which two feminist literary critics questioned the unexamined assumptions of most theoretical approaches to literature. The first was Ellen Messer-Davidow's "The Philosophical Bases of Feminist Literary Criticisms" (1987). Here Messer-Davidow offered a detailed discussion of the origins of feminist criticism and the assumptions that it challenges. She argues that various kinds of critiques (feminist, race, class) are necessary for advancing literary critical understanding. However, she also sees a choice that critics must make: either to balance between traditional and feminist, etc., criticism, which she thinks are "fundamentally incompatible," or to "transform [critical methodology] into one of our own making" and "reconstitute literary study."[19] All of this is still very "theoretical," though, and seems to advocate yet another -ism to be imposed on a text.

In the second essay, published in 1989, Jane Tompkins took up Messer-Davidow's critique of conventional literary criticism, recalling her own early career, when she thought that women should "get theory" in order to get into "the big leagues" and argue with men on their own terms (25). However, by the time she wrote "Me and My Shadow," she considered that "theory itself . . . may be one of the patriarchal gestures women *and* men ought to avoid" (25). In other words, a theory is *still* theory. Why should women have to argue with men on men's terms only? Because "To break with the convention is to risk not being heard at all" (26). In 1990, Olivia Frey agreed, arguing that women practice conventional criticism because they are anxious about being taken seriously (57).

Personal criticism has evolved from this anxiety and from the desire to express one's own ideas outside the boundaries of conventional criticism. Rachel Brownstein devoted a whole book, *Becoming a Heroine: Reading about Women in Novels* (1982), to understanding how one reader, Brownstein herself, understood the heroines in nineteenth-century novels. She asserted that reading can matter in one's life, but the text must be taken seriously, *personally* ("Interrupted Reading: Personal Criticism in the Present Time" 33). Frances Murphy Zauhar took that argument a step further by comparing how literary critics are supposed to relate to books: "Mainstream literary criticism has, until very recently, reinforced the convention that the 'good' reader remains detached from the reading, unaffected in a moral or developmental sense; and only under those conditions is he (or sometimes she) able to make a responsible assessment of the text at hand" (106). This approach represents a dubious attempt to read a book objectively, whereas most of us react subjectively and emotionally, and in fact "most literature was meant to be read by a totally engaged, emotionally involved reader" (107). This is the reader that Bessie Head wants.

---

19  Later, in an assessment of personal criticism ("Autocritique"), Candace Lang stated that critics need to define their own "presuppositions, methodological tools, and consequences of those choices" (43–44).

A similar problem of perspective exists regarding African literature and African critics.[20] After twenty years living in Southern Africa, I am still struck by the nature of the personal investment that most African writers and critics have in their societies. This is sometimes understood by non-Africans as producing didactic (meaning "simple" or "not complex") literature or, more generously, activist literature. But as a former teacher at an African university and as a critic of local literatures in English in Botswana, I have come to appreciate the pedagogical aspect of African literature that enhances its appeal to African readers in a way that Western literature does not.[21] Students always want to know what "message" a text (whether poem, prose, or play) conveys, what they can learn about their lives from their reading. (Incidentally, this pedagogical aspect has deep roots in the oral traditions still strong in most Southern African societies.)

Bessie Head recognized this aspect too: in *A Question of Power*, Elizabeth overhears the Danish worker Camilla announcing that "'[i]n our country culture has become so complex, this complexity is reflected in our literature. It takes a certain level of education to understand our novelists. The ordinary man cannot understand them. . .'" (79, ellipsis in original). Elizabeth is puzzled: "It never occurred to her that those authors had ceased to be of any value whatsoever to their society—or was it really true that an extreme height of culture and the incomprehensible went hand in hand?" (79). Yes, well, there we are.

My purpose is neither personal criticism (called "confessional criticism" by its detractors) nor theoretical or ideological rigor. My personal observations are not intended as confessions but as examples of how one reader relates to one writer. Theory cannot address this relationship because of its very nature, because of its ideological uniformity. My analyses will more closely approximate Messer-Davidow's perspectivism, but I will not claim that my

---

20 I have written elsewhere about the issue of Western critics acknowledging their own biases when writing about African literature. See *Novels of Botswana in English, 1930–2006*, pp. 5–7 and 90.
21 In "The Novelist as Teacher," Chinua Achebe writes about his role in reeducating people about their own culture, a responsibility felt by many African writers, given what colonial conquest did to Africa, but Achebe also addresses the role of literature in providing life lessons, citing several readers who would wish him to help them learn those lessons. He also makes the point, however, that he is not that sort of writer.

perspective is authoritative, since I believe that all perspectives on Bessie Head, including mine, are mutable and very fluid.

As I wrote my dissertation on Bessie Head, I found that all my fixed notions about what her books were about went into a kind of flux, and much of what I thought about the world changed; nevertheless, I wrote what I was expected to write (being one example of Frey's anxious woman critic). As I reread that dissertation many years later, I found that the same thing had happened in the intervening years: all my new fixed notions about what her books were about went into a kind of flux again. I am not alone in this experience of reading Bessie Head. Tom Holzinger wrote at the end of his memoir "Conversations and Consternations with B Head," "Coming to the end of these recollections, I am once more uneasy. B Head is a force of nature with myriad forms. I'm afraid I know her in only a few of them. She may well hate these pages and call me a damn blasted liar. But please, Bessie, be patient with me one last time; I have done what I can" (57).

Desiree Lewis summarizes what is perhaps the greatest challenge to reading Bessie Head's work: the impossibility of classifying it in any meaningful, tidy, easily accessible way.

> Much of the reading that *does* focus on the substance of her writing tends to continue an appropriating impulse. Head is read in terms of what the reader would like to see: the feminist writer who consistently subverts masculine authority (even though Head often celebrated masculinity and authoritative male leaders). Or the socially committed writer who identifies clear-cut solutions to oppression (although Head was often preoccupied with spiritual sources and forms of liberation). Or the politically incorrect writer who "failed" to sustain a feminist critique or social commitment (even though she probed injustices in extremely expansive ways). Or the writer of "essentially African" works, (despite the fact that she developed a universal vision and also drew self-consciously on writers like Boris Paserna[k] and DH Lawrence). ("Bessie Head's Freedoms")

Critics like to label texts and thus make them their "own," but in her character, in her letters, and in every aspect of her life, Bessie Head resisted attempts to label things, so that people who talked with her, read her letters or other writing, or even just saw her passing on the street found it difficult to get a fix on her.[22] I think there might be some value in beginning with some kind of framework, since it gives a point of approach, a point of common interest that might, in the end, take the reader or critic in an entirely different direction.

But "getting a fix" on a text is what literary criticism has in recent decades been about: the idea that a theoretical model (Marxism, deconstruction, modernism, etc.) can be used to analyze and understand a literary text; certainly this approach defines my own education. Theoretical models have been applied as well to Bessie Head's texts, but with less success. To assume that a single model can somehow explain the work of someone who categorically rejected all forms of categorization is to overlook the richness and complexity of that work. Sarah Mandow describes the situation as follows, by drawing comparisons with the structural "difficulty" of *A Question of Power*:

> [T]o read at the borderline of fiction and chronicle, with no conventional boundaries, is like entering Elizabeth's mind; the seemingly formal third-person narrative serves to heighten the depersonalisation of her mental invasion and offers no refuge for the reader . . . Because the reader is implicated in the experiences the text conveys, the process of interpreting the text . . . creates a feeling in the reader of having her own mind invaded. (154)

What Mandow describes here is in fact more than the dialogue that Desiree Lewis sees in Head's writing: it is an identification with the experiences of both the character and the writer, an identification that makes interpretation difficult without the kind of self-examination that I believe is intrinsic to a proper reading of all Head's work.[23]

Mandow's analysis of the way *A Question of Power* affects readers also gets to the heart of why so much Bessie Head criticism seems so unsatisfying to me: no matter how convincing an argument may be, it still seems untenable. Or, as Tom Holzinger wrote, Head "was herself a contradiction, and she had an acute sense of tension in life and thought" ("Conversations and Consternations with B Head" 40). So to apply a model to something written by Bessie Head,

22 See Tom Holzinger, "Conversations and Consternations with B Head," for a personal recollection of some of the many facets of Bessie Head's personality.
23 See David Kerr, "Character, Role, Madness, God, Biography, Narrative: Dismantling and Reassembling Bessie Head's *A Question of Power*," for a discussion of the experience of workshopping a play based on Bessie Head's work.

she who ignored and rejected models, seems in the end inadequate, or even worse, inappropriate.

For a long time, and following the sanctioned discipline of applying critical models, most criticism of Head's work identified with one of the categories that Lewis enumerates above: feminist, sociopolitical, African or postcolonial, as well as psychological. Feminist critiques of Head raised useful questions regarding the way Head perceived herself as a writer, but since she did not consider herself a feminist and indeed rejected the tenets of feminism—in favor of a much broader vision of what it means to be a human being with choices about our lives—such critiques neglected that aspect of her philosophy. She refused, for example, to repudiate what she considered the masculine sides of herself, choosing instead to embrace all her characteristics and to assert both their masculinity and their importance. However, Head did recognize the male–female conflicts in the society around her, and her reflections on that conflict and its consequences certainly appear in her fiction, especially the consequences of power residing with men.

Feminist readings of her work, however, tended to focus only on the conflict and to neglect the representations of positive masculinity that are inevitably present, as well as the trend toward a more general understanding of why male–female conflicts arise. Statements such as the following demonstrate this desire to appropriate Head for the feminist cause. Charlotte Bruner, for example, wrote that "[e]xcept for her son, the portraits of male figures become increasingly threatening in Head's work" (270), overlooking Makhaya, Gilbert, Tom, Eugene, Sello, Sebina (in *A Bewitched Crossroad*), and male characters in the short stories, such as Paul Thebolo. Nancy Topping Bazin stated that "men degrade, manipulate and abuse women" in Elizabeth's madness ("Weight of Custom" 187), but they also give her love. Bazin also wrote that "Head [chooses] to focus on sexism rather than racism in *A Question of Power*" ("Venturing into Feminist Consciousness" 56). However, Head does not focus on one more than the other; the legacy of white racism evident in characters like Camilla is only a part of the problem. The tormentors are as much African as they are male, and much of the torment reflects the attitude that Elizabeth (or Margaret Cadmore Junior, for that matter) is not only "just" a woman but is also not properly African. Finally, Femi Ojo-Ade stated flatly that "Bessie

Head does not concern herself with questions of feminism" (15)—perhaps a true statement—but said that this was because the African woman "has never been considered shackled by any means" (14), whereas Head herself wrote in the short story "The Collector of Treasures" that "[t]he ancestors made so many errors and one of the most bitter-making things was that they relegated to men a superior position in the tribe, while women were regarded, in a congenital sense, as being an inferior form of human life" (92). By placing Head so firmly on one side or the other of the feminist divide, such readings missed the uncertainty that Head's fiction captures so well and from which arise new ways of discovery and appreciation. That uncertainty is central to the experience of reading and engaging with her.

Several feminist critics addressed the fact that Head was writing her own story, and certainly the autobiographical aspects are central to reading Bessie Head's writing,[24] but the importance of how Head integrated everything into her life and her work means that it is also true that Head's vision is not as narrow as her own life—or perhaps that any life is not as narrow as a vision.

Political critiques are unsatisfying because of Head's oft-quoted statement that "political camps falsify truth" ("Some Notes on Novel Writing" 63), a protestation borne out by the fact that nearly all attempts to classify her work run up against inconsistency. Head's fiction is necessarily political because of the background against which she wrote, but again, because of her own disavowal of any political creed, those who would wish to read her work in an explicitly political framework find little to satisfy them (remember that her "home" is "where the wind don't blow"). It is true that she wrote in the context of a very politically volatile time in the history of African literature: independence and immediate postindependence invited many, if not most, African writers to deal with questions of postcolonial identity, the place of tradition in independent African societies, or the issue of ethnicity in relation to national identity.[25] As Lewis points out in "Bessie Head's Freedoms," Head was often seen as a

---

24  See Jane Bryce-Okunlola and Caroline Rooney.
25  Simon Gikandi wrote that modern African literature has been indelibly shaped by the colonial encounter, but further, that "[i]t was at this point [independence]—the point where western notions about nature, culture, and self were turned against the project of colonialism—that the largest body of work by African writers was produced" (385). Bessie Head certainly did not follow this pattern.

"failed" writer in this context, most notably by Lewis Nkosi, who dismissed her characters as insufficiently engaged with the problems of the African, in particular the South African, struggle for freedom ("Southern Africa: Protest and Commitment"). In fact, of course, the struggle for freedom, or "whatever illusion of freedom lay ahead" (*When Rain Clouds Gather*[26] 1) in the future, was one of her most pressing concerns: this freedom could only be achieved through a detailed scrutiny of both social and personal forces that led to oppression of all people, and not through support of a particular ideology.

Kolawole Ogungbesan and Isabella Matsikidze are two of the earliest critics who saw the possibility for a different approach. Ogungbesan noted that Head was one of the few African writers who did not "equate the achievement of individuality with the process of alienation" (211); instead, argued Ogungbesan, she shows how achievement of individual awareness brings people (exiles and outsiders, in Ogungbesan's argument) into community with each other and strengthens a particular social system. Matsikidze wrote about the imagined future of *Maru*, one "where 'goodness, compassion, justice and truth' reign, which Head desires to make accessible for Southern Africa. How shall this utopia be achieved? That is the problem of Head's politics. It is ultimately idealistic. Yet to say that she is politically ignorant because her proposals are not practical is, I think, a misreading of her art" ("Toward a Redemptive Political Philosophy" 106). Maria Olaussen takes that notion even further, and her ideas will be discussed below.

Psychological criticism tends to be the most unsatisfactory approach to reading Bessie Head. Diagnosing Elizabeth's disorder(s) might be interesting, but it diminishes the force and consequences of real abuse. Sarah Mandow, again, takes issue particularly with Patrick Colm Hogan's study of *A Question of Power* as "a Lacanian psychosis": by insisting that the novel is not autobiographical, Hogan can comfortably perform an analysis of the book's psychosis (152), but he ends up "doing what Bessie Head herself draws attention to when she condemns another of her critics as portraying her as 'a mentally ill writer who wrote mentally ill books' (qtd. in Eilersen, *Thunder*

---

26  All quotations from *When Rain Clouds Gather* and *Maru* come from the 2010 Virago combined edition of these novels, although they will be identified by the individual titles.

256)" (152). Because *A Question of Power* is autobiographical, many critics transfer literary analysis to Bessie Head herself; this transfer is what Mandow takes issue with. Bessie Head undoubtedly had episodes of mental illness, and she herself was aware of that aspect of her experiences; that much is clear from reading her letters. But to diagnose her through her books is pointless. It is also pointless to diagnose Elizabeth, since what happens to Elizabeth is fictional, created by Bessie Head out of her own experiences, but also shaped by her to make a greater point.

Elizabeth Evasdaughter, in "Bessie Head's *A Question of Power* Read as a Mariner's Guide to Paranoia," used the *Diagnostic and Statistical Manual of Mental Disorders* to demonstrate that Elizabeth suffers from paranoid schizophrenia and then showed that her illness is a reaction to power. Evasdaughter failed to consider the possibility that schizophrenia might be an incomplete assessment of Elizabeth. Adetokunbo Pearse offered a similar reading: his analysis is more classically Freudian (he categorizes Elizabeth's experiences according to conscious, subconscious, and unconscious), and his conclusions are essentially the same. But, again, given the spiritual character of her "hallucinations," it is important to consider other evaluations of Elizabeth's behavior in order to derive meaning from *A Question of Power*.

One of the most interesting readings of Head to emerge from this period is Modupe Olaogun's "Irony and Schizophrenia in Bessie Head's *Maru*." Olaogun presented a reading of *Maru* that connects the literary device of irony, which arises from the potential of double meanings, to the psychiatric evaluation of schizophrenia, which Olaogun understood as also arising from double— and contradictory—meanings. Such an analysis opens up other possibilities for reading Head's writing because it assumes the importance of uncertainty, rather than dismissing it as a structural flaw.

Maria Olaussen's 1997 study *Forceful Creation in Harsh Terrain* was probably the first critical evaluation to admit the necessity of contradiction in Bessie Head's philosophy. Olaussen's central focus is to study the movement from placelessness to place in *When Rain Clouds Gather*, *Maru*, and *A Question of Power*. That physical movement, she argues, refers at the same time to a movement from questions of identity to questions of community (14, and referring to Craig MacKenzie): the human being wandering from place to place is trying to find an identity that exists within a community. We establish our unique self by confronting and interacting with others. Here, for perhaps the first time, is an open identification of the necessity for contradiction and even impossibility in Bessie Head's work: Olaussen wrote that "Head's fiction shows how the ideal of the individual as representative of a larger common universal humanity is a necessary but problematic ideal" (37); in other words, to say that someone is a representative of humanity is to emphasize the characteristics they *share* with others, but in fact it is simultaneously necessary for that person to set herself *apart* from others. An example of the problems inherent in this ideal comes in the final pages of *Maru*, when Maru marries Margaret and removes her from the village from which she has drawn her creative inspiration, and also where her best friend and her first love live. Even that famous "gesture of belonging" demonstrates the difficulty of achieving that ideal. In these examples, a person's most valuable contribution comes only after she has been removed from society.

What Olaussen believes, in the way that Head's most important characters remain outside the community, is that Head is aiming for universality from outside, rather than universalizing from within (148). What this means is that universality is something to strive for, a movement towards the outside of oneself, rather than the sameness of universalism imposed from inside, in the reverse of the common perception. The dangers of the latter are suggested in the way the threats move progressively closer to the protagonist in the three novels: in *When Rain Clouds Gather*, the dualism of good and evil is completely external to Makhaya, although he can recognize it; it moves much closer to Margaret Cadmore in the figure of her future husband Maru (and she herself even experiences brief moments of it when, for example, she imagines that she is killing one of the pupils who is taunting her [258]); it finally invades Elizabeth completely in *A Question of Power*, in the figure of Sello, who is "both God and the Devil at the same time" (176). One reader noted the encroachment in the way that goats are portrayed in the three novels: in *When Rain Clouds Gather*, a goat visits George Appleby-Smith's office regularly for a year (208), and Gilbert notices that the goats would like to stop and talk, but they are in a hurry (29). In *Maru*, the goats invade Margaret Cadmore's house, soiling it and creating havoc with visitors (although they are friendly to Margaret herself); the kid is eventually traumatized by the slaughter of its mother.[27] In *A Question of Power*, the goats simply fall off the end of the earth (95).

Olaussen concludes that "[t]he universal for Head is both a way of connecting to the specific and a way of escaping from it" (183). Makhaya, for example, is able to join the community of Golema Mmidi (itself a "community" of outsiders, of people who are not related to one another, not typical of Tswana villages) by entering into a traditional relationship, marriage, but with a very un-traditional woman (259). His sense of himself, his security, and his sense of possibilities come from limitations—marriage, family, commitments—the ultimate limit (or perhaps the ultimate possibility?) being death (262).

In the context of the search for "freedom," Head's characters must always come to terms with their limitations and with the unsolvable contradictions inherent to human life. Once the ideologies are abandoned, in favor of facing and endlessly negotiating the contradictions, the richness of Head's ideas begins to become clear. It is a richness that is not bound by any given period in history or any phase of any human life, whether the reader's or the character's. Neither history and politics (the general) nor individual psychology (the specific) is sufficient to eliminate oppression, but instead both, and neither, and sometimes at the same time. Perhaps these impossibilities can only be understood in a context of some kind of faith, one that we must look for when we read the trilogy *When Rain Clouds Gather*, *Maru*, and *A Question of Power*. It is said that wisdom comes from understanding the opposite of something, and even perhaps knowing it. Elizabeth can only survive after she has seen and even been evil. Her struggle with God is difficult because the "right to self-determination" (Olaussen 40) is expressed as identification with God/Creator, who is also the being to whom all human beings are supposed to submit themselves. How can identification with and submission to another lead to self-determination?

Sarah Mandow, in a provocative reading of *A Question of Power*, suggests that the very structure of this novel makes it impossible for any reader to find

---

27 Eilersen points out that goats wandered in and out of Bessie Head's house while she was writing *Maru* (*Thunder behind Her Ears* 134).

a sympathetic character to grab hold of, but that this is the genius of Head's writing. *A Question of Power*, Mandow asserts, is not comfortable to read or to write about because of how it blurs divisions, most obviously between Elizabeth and Bessie Head, but also in how the reader is drawn into the world of the novel. Bessie Head "deepens" arguments by defining (and defending) both sides of an issue. And as the novel, or Elizabeth, or Bessie Head, slips from one side to the other, she takes her readers, and her critics, with her: "The merging of autobiography and fiction, the way inner and outer realities merge within the novel, seems compelled to be repeated in critics' responses" (151).

Thus it seems to me that the most honest way to read *A Question of Power* is to engage with it personally (as Rachel Brownstein advocates). For Mandow, the merging of autobiography and fiction happens in the novel most clearly in the use of "the seemingly formal third-person narrative" that "serves to heighten the depersonalisation of her mental invasion and offers no refuge for the reader" (154): we think we are safe from what happens to Elizabeth because the narrator offers us a veneer of objective distance, but it is one that we realize has deceived us when we are suddenly dumped into the "other" world—external or internal—without any warning at all. *A Question of Power* is about Bessie Head herself, but it is also not; it is about us more generally.

More generally, I agree with Mandow because for me, this statement and her discussion more generally mean that it is difficult, if not impossible, not to take Bessie Head personally. Mandow herself identifies the importance of being personal:

> There is no comfortable place from which to begin to write about Bessie Head and her work. For me the reason is partly, to borrow from the opening sentence of *A Question of Power*, that although "it may seem almost incidental that I am not African," my position as a white western feminist studying an African woman's text is one of crucial significance. The full import of that borrowed line resides in the "almost": a near-erasure of a crucial distinction that, were I to ignore it, would lead to a repetition of the abuses of power that the novel lays bare. (147)

As I noted earlier, in the reader-response model, we bring our selves to the text, but when reading Bessie Head, our involvement in what she writes about means that we come away not only guilty and innocent, but different, a little transformed each time. You have to think about who you are when you read Bessie Head.

Desiree Lewis's *Living on a Horizon*, published in 2007, shows how Head exposes universal patterns of power through personal and social relationships because she "avoids the progressive political models" (2) of the 1960s, 1970s, and 1980s. During that time, much literature from South Africa as well as the rest of Africa articulated struggles for autonomy but from particular ideological perspectives (communism, socialism, Marxism, nationalism, etc.). Lewis wrote that in Head, "criticism is forced to confront its limitations" (7).[28] The difficulty of "criticism" thus becomes clear.

Lewis believes that Head's works "defy conclusive interpretation" (15). Instead, she wrote, Head "allows contradictions to function in arresting and imaginative ways" (4). In other words, the best way to "get into" Bessie Head is to accept the contradictions and problems in her texts. For Olaussen, solving those contradictions—that cannot in any case be reconciled—is to destroy meaning. Accepting the contradictions is not an easy thing to do. Lewis wrote that Head "painfully explores and unravels, constantly upending her abstruse 'conclusions' at the same time that she struggles to articulate them" (7) and therefore that Head's works "illustrate her manoeuvre of generating a broad critical standpoint from immediate personal experiences" (19). In this way, argues Lewis, Head exposes universal patterns of power by examining, well, everything about her own life and the lives of those around her.

The nature of Head's work is such that polar opposites must coexist: all the characters demonstrate both good and evil characteristics, and identifying them as representatives of a particular polarity ignores Head's own tendency toward something else. Linda-Susan Beard wrote that "[t]he fundamental absolute to be dismantled, of course, is the myth of polarity" ("Bessie Head's *A Question of Power*" 268). Jean Marquard also noted the parallel development in *A Question of Power* of "the new schemes of values . . . located in the

---

28 Gillian Brown wrote more generally of personal criticism that "[d]rawing attention to individual experience, the critic underscores the particularity as well as partiality of any critical view. From this perspective, the invocation of a personal experience is a confession of critical limits, of one's bias or ignorance or historical horizon" (107); however she worries that "confession can amount to a claim of critical authority based upon one's very limitations" (107).

mind of a single character" and "the ideal garden . . . once again cultivated on a co-operative basis" (60).[29] Beard and Marquard pointed the way to an "unfinished" reading of Bessie Head, one that is articulated most clearly today by Mandow, Olaussen, and Lewis.

Finally, in the past ten years or so, eco-critics have begun to address the natural and agricultural imagery in Head's work. The significance of this imagery was noted earlier, of course, in terms of how landscape not only alienated the characters but also held within it the possibility for self-definition and rejuvenation.[30] In 2008, Sonja Darlington situated Bessie Head's writing more firmly within the emerging principles of eco-criticism, noting that Head's nature metaphors are "full of complexities" (53).[31]

These complexities, however, go beyond the natural and agricultural metaphors. Tswana land-settlement patterns are fairly unusual,[32] and Golema Mmidi is not a typical, traditional, Tswana village. It is a village made up of outsiders who have left more traditional villages in order to build new lives and a new society for themselves. Head created Golema Mmidi in a particular place and time—Botswana at the point of independence—that need to be understood and accounted for in order to understand those complexities. Head doesn't just observe the society and the farms and the landscape: she watches people and animals interact with her garden in Serowe, and describes an integrated whole. We can study Head's gardens as places or objects, but the vines touch nearly every aspect of human life, and that is when things get opened up.

---

29 Marquard alludes to Voltaire's *Candide*, in which the ideal garden is a very problematic answer to the difficulties of human existence.

30 See, e.g., Jean Marquard, "The Farm: A Concept in the Writing of Olive Schreiner, Pauline Smith, Doris Lessing, Nadine Gordimer and Bessie Head"; Maxine Sample, "Landscape and Spatial Metaphor in Bessie Head's *The Collector of Treasures*"; Victoria Margree, "Wild Flowers: Bessie Head on Life, Health and Botany"; and Anissa Talahite, "Cape Gooseberries and Giant Cauliflowers: Transplantation, Hybridity, and Growth in Bessie Head's *A Question of Power*."

31 See also Sonja Darlington, "The Significance of Bessie Head's Response to 'The Call of the Global Green'"; William Slaymaker, "Echoing the Other(s): The Call of the Global Green and Black African Responses"; Elspeth Tulloch, "Husbandry, Agriculture and Ecocide: Reading Bessie Head's *When Rain Clouds Gather* as a Postcolonial Georgic"; and Dokubo Melford Goodhead, "The Discourse of Sustainable Farming and the Environment in Bessie Head's *When Rain Clouds Gather*."

32 See R. M. K. Siletshena, "Migration and Permanent Settlement at the Lands Area," for more information about Tswana land settlement.

The multiple perspectives of personal criticism can be useful for understanding a writer like Bessie Head, whose "unfinished," open structure invites personal interaction and interfacing differently from other writers. Head engages readers in the way that Frances Murphy Zauhar identifies, not just making them feel empathy for her characters but forcing them to recognize patterns and forces at work in their own lives. This is a kind of personal reading that is less confessional than it is revelatory. Whatever epiphanies I experience through the medium of Head's writing encompass more than just revealing things about myself: I am also interested in how those epiphanies happen and how my reading evolves. I do not wish to fall into the confessional aspects of that style. Charles Altieri wrote that he does "not see much point to autobiography for lives like . . . mine, where in fact the shaping events are so common" (65). I do not wish to confess, nor to write my own autobiography. Every life is in and of itself important, but the issue is what literature can do to a life, how it can affect that life. So this book is also not about me, but about how reading Bessie Head changes this particular reader over time.

\* \* \*

Enter a gathering of Bessie Head scholars, and you discover that we refer to her simply as Bessie, despite that many of us never knew her.[33] We quote our favorite passages repeatedly. We laugh out loud at her jokes and wit. We giggle nervously at her diatribes. We reread everything we can get our hands on. We celebrate her birthday. We protect her legacy.

This is hardly the detached, objective style preferred by conventional criticism.

Living and working in Botswana, meeting people she knew and was friends with, and becoming part of that group mentioned above (even helping to foster it), reading the Bessie Head Papers in the reading room[34] at the Khama

---

33 For one Head scholar, this use of the first name raises an important issue concerning how forms of address show respect or disrespect for black women. My own use varies, even in this book. In Serowe, she was MmaHead (sort of like Mrs. Head, pronounced "MmaHeady") or MmaHoward (mother of Howard) or simply Bessie, all of which are quite respectful in Botswana. In discussions, she apparently sometimes referred to herself in the third person, as B Head (usually with an unspoken exclamation mark). She signed her letters variously as "Bessie Head," "Bessie," or "Bess," depending on degree of familiarity. I call her Bessie because her writing is intense and extremely personal.

34 The small, brightly sunlit reading room is next to the vault where the papers are stored, in a small, four-room building, known as the white house, next to the main museum building, the red house. The white house opens onto the museum courtyard, which is planted with grass and trees and

III Memorial Museum in Serowe, has changed my opinion about many things "Bessie." She is no longer just a great writer. She is a person who had a life here and left bits of herself behind in the people she knew and the books she wrote. Analyzing those books in a more strictly literary critical way seems like an intrusion, and comes too close to performing some kind of autopsy on Bessie herself, and the mess is ugly. I worry about what she would think of me. I do not worry about that with any other writer.

When I wrote my original dissertation, I looked at as much material as I could find, but looking at the dissertation fifteen years later, I found that I was utterly dissatisfied with much of it. I have lived here long enough to know that I am hardly an expert, that my life here and my relationships with people and my work teaching here have fundamentally changed how I think about literary analysis and its relationship to life.

I am dissatisfied with much Bessie Head criticism. I think this stems in part from my evolving disaffection with literary criticism in general, because it seems to me to fail to capture what I imagine drew most people to the study of literature in the first place. What I would like to do in this book is to recover the sense of joy that brought me to literature, a joy that is certainly reflected in Head's writing, to look at my response to Bessie Head as her manipulated drawing-out of my own desire for something greater than myself, to respond to Head the writer of the books, and to leave a whole lot of questions unanswered, because that is the way people are: unanswered and unsolvable.

The place that Head eventually finds for Elizabeth contains certain utopian aspects, but they are not utopian exclusively in a social sense. Order, institutions, and ideology must, in Head's world, be inadequate, since they propose exactly the kind of structure that is opposed to Head's own vision, which is as unstructured as love. If the utopian community is ordered by human relationships, then love is a central component of Head's definition of utopia. It is not the Garden of Eden (or even Voltaire's garden) because Head's God lives within the garden *as* all human members. Utopia, defined in terms

---

inhabited by chickens, foraging for seeds, that occasionally wander into the white house. It is difficult to imagine a better repository for the letters because of the "ordinariness" and friendliness of the place. Life happens there.

of love, exists in people and as their network of relationships: it is no place, but all people.

At this point, I need to address the possibility that the following extended discussion/essay/discourse will not be very tidy and will probably in fact be rather unwieldy. I remember when I was a graduate student in German, and two colleagues from a seminar on the modern novel decided that they were going to write a paper analyzing Franz Kafka's *Das Schloß* (The Castle). I can no longer remember the topic of their paper, but I do remember that the more they looked at it in order to tidy up the loose ends, the more loose ends they created, the longer the paper became, and the more impossible their project of producing any kind of complete paper.[35] To some extent, this impossibility is characteristic of all great literature, but in the case of Kafka, it is probably a defining one. After a year, numerous extensions, and a long-standing "Incomplete," the professor told them to just turn their paper in and all would be well. And still they had trouble letting go. The image of them hunched over a desk, the sound of despair in their voices as they realized that solving one analytical problem meant creating another one, and remembering the way in which Kafka consumed their existence for that year (he would, wouldn't he?) looms in my mind now as I consider my own consuming passion for Bessie Head's writing. I will not pretend to offer any kind of completeness here. Head's writing is more like a path with many branches, and every time I read something of hers I seem to end up in a different place, different from where I was last time and always different from what I expected. I grope in the half-illuminated text, stumbling onto insights, but then realizing that the road doesn't lead where it did last time. I feel like Gilbert Balfour, in *When Rain Clouds Gather*, who never could unravel the mysteries of the paths through the bush that the villagers navigated so easily:

> [T]he bush belonged to all the Batswana people, who had created its footpaths and mapped out its length and breadth in their minds. It had often amazed him to discover that cattlemen drove their cattle home, through the bush, in pitch darkness, with an unerring sense of direction, while he,

---

35 I am also, but less vividly, reminded of David Lodge's character Morris Zapp, who is endlessly writing his comprehensive work on Jane Austen.

Gilbert, had several times lost his direction within the fenced farm lands, and his legs and arms bore lots of scars from having pitched himself into a barbed-wire fence at night. (182)

*A Question of Power* opens up the possibility, already identified in *When Rain Clouds Gather* and *Maru*, that human potential exists in the intersection of *all* aspects of human life, in *all* ways of knowing, because as human beings, we must lay claim to our selves, our communities, and the intangible understanding that comes from our souls. We must enter Bessie Head's world because we are already there—innocent, guilty, wonderful, and always endlessly possible.

2

# "The Woman . . . Is No Neurotic"

*May I ask you to remove two words from your thesis, <u>neurotic</u> and <u>madness</u> for Elizabeth of <u>Question</u>? I told you I loved your thesis on my work to the point of abject worship. The only two words I have objection to in the thesis are <u>neurotic</u> and <u>madness</u>. The woman who stands by the kitchen sink and laughs so richly and superbly while Tom washes, is no neurotic; the vigorous vegetable gard[e]ner is no neurotic; the vigorous author of <u>Question</u> is no inward-turning neurotic. Secondly, <u>Question</u>, split readers and reviewers into two camps. The first camp said: This is a magnificent account of insanity. The second camp said: Because of the book's essential wisdom, it is a pity she does not have control over the experience. The second camp is near the truth. The truth is that I could see so far and no further.*

KMM 72 BHP 10, July 27, 1983, to Jane Bryce

*"Tell me one last thing," said Harry. "Is this real? Or has this been happening inside my head?"*

*Dumbledore beamed at him, and his voice sounded loud and strong in Harry's ears even though the bright mist was descending again, obscuring his figure.*

*"Of course it is happening inside your head, Harry, but why on earth should that mean that it is not real?"*

J. K. Rowling, *Harry Potter and the Deathly Hallows* 579

When Harry Potter, in the seventh book of J. K. Rowling's series, asks his mentor Professor Dumbledore about the reality of their mental meeting, Harry has apparently just been killed by Lord Voldemort. At the moment of his "death," Harry finds that instead of being in the Forbidden Forest adjacent to Hogwarts (where he went to meet Voldemort and to allow Voldemort to kill him), he is in King's Cross station in London. King's Cross is important generally as a hub of transportation to other places outside London—in this case, the hereafter—but it is also important for Harry symbolically because it is where he left the world of Muggles for the first time and found his purpose and his happiness, not just as a wizard but as a human being. When I read this passage from _The Deathly Hallows_, I was immediately reminded of _A Question of Power_. That, I thought, is the central problem with criticism of _A Question of Power_. The question to ask is not whether it is all happening inside Elizabeth's head: it is, and it is also happening outside her head. In fact, it can be argued[1] that what happens inside her head spills over in very "real" ways into the "real" world.

For example, at one point, when Tom and Elizabeth are having a conversation, Sello interjects: "'Yes, that's right,' and off went the chair with a loud 'ting'. Tom started and looked about the room with wide, alert eyes: 'Did you hear something?' he said quickly. 'I distinctly heard someone say "yes, that's right"': and he kept very still, his eyes roving curiously around the room" (_A Question of Power_ 24). Later, Elizabeth's son asks her about some burn marks on the bedroom floor:

> She jumped up alarmed. Why, anything could happen in her nightmare. She might have left a cigarette lit. She walked to the door of her bedroom, then froze. There was the drama of a death-throe on the floor. Charcoal-like footprints dragged into each other across the floor and in the centre of the room was a heap of charcoal dust. She half muttered aloud to herself:
>
> "Is this the last of Medusa?"
>
> From the room behind her Sello said: "Yes."
>
> "What are you saying?" the small boy asked. (_A Question of Power_ 93)

So if all of these things happen "outside" her mind, any analysis that begins with assumptions regarding Elizabeth's sanity are getting on the wrong train. _A Question of Power_ is a work of fiction, so madness cannot be a pathological issue, only a literary one.

What Bessie Head seems to be aiming for is simultaneously a challenge to the status quo and a general attempt to understand the "truth" about our own

---

1 Craig Mackenzie also identifies this "irruption of the imaginary into the real" (153), citing the same two examples.

lives. For Elizabeth, and I think for Head as well, that truth can only come from a very thorough and critical—in the sense of honest—examination of the role of self, society, and spirituality. It is not so much that Elizabeth is mad, but that she is engaged in a very private dialogue about the nature of good and evil in herself. Bessie Head was engaged in a very public dialogue about the same thing. If we as readers take her on, accept her invitation, and accept Elizabeth's madness as real, then we too must ask ourselves the same, or at least similar, questions about the nature of good and evil in ourselves and how we can truly love (or worship[2]) other people. Because we each live different lives and because the consequences of our decisions, both personal and social, remain for a very long time, our answers might not be the same as Elizabeth's, Head's, or anyone else's, but we must grapple with the questions nonetheless.

In this chapter, I want to think about what madness means in terms of a person's psychic, emotional, and intellectual life. When I wrote my dissertation, I concluded that oppression makes people mad. Yes, well, I can say that these questions still interest me, but I know that my earlier conclusion was too simple. Before I can consider the aspects of Head's books that have so directly impacted my life, I have to consider the difference between the external and internal aspects of life.

In my original dissertation, I looked at the writings of Ruth Benedict, an anthropologist, R. D. Laing, a psychotherapist, and Michel Foucault, a philosopher. Benedict offered explanations about basic patterns of societal development; both Laing and Foucault examined the social construction of madness and the function and uses of madness within a society. At the time, I argued that Elizabeth's madness had been brought on by the intolerable pressures of an intolerable society, and that Elizabeth must move through the experiences in order to become a true prophet. Now, more than twenty years later, the first aspect seems obvious—in the literary meaning of the novel, not in the pathological sense—and the second one seems incorrect. A new aspect, the private one between reader, writer, and character, seems more significant.

---

2  In a letter to Betty Fradkin (KMM 15 BHP 21, February 4, 1976), Bessie Head wrote that "I'd sort of refer to a man I might love as a God but I mean by that that love is basically worship of another person." Later, in a letter to Gloria Joseph, she repeated this notion: "I never love. I only worship" (KMM 41 BHP 11, May 4, 1981).

The important point is not so much that Bessie Head recognized that apartheid did not allow for full development of the individual; clearly it was designed not to. Elizabeth is named as a prophet at the end of *A Question of Power*, but a prophet of what? Bessie Head eschewed all forms of ideology, including and perhaps especially political ones. Her "Truth" is the truth that exists between human beings in their relationships to each other.

When I first reread my dissertation, Laing seemed inappropriate because psychoanalytic theory had long since moved on; his ideas were probably even outdated at the time I originally wrote, and after rereading I thought I ought to remove him. After all, nothing I had read gave any indication that Bessie Head herself had any exposure to either Laing or Foucault, not that it made any difference in the practice of literary criticism, in the exercise of writing a dissertation, but earlier I was performing the kind of literary exercise that I now object to, and that Bessie Head herself certainly would have objected to: applying a theoretical model to a literary text with no basis for doing so. And yet, Laing made sense somehow.

Then, when I was up in Serowe in March 2011 to go through the letters in a more detailed and systematic way than I had yet done, I came across a letter from Betsy Wood letting Head know that "[o]ur son in Los Angeles found the book you had hoped for—by R. D. Laing. It came yesterday! And I'm putting it in the post for you" (KMM 9 BHP 9, April 16, n.y.). In another letter from Beata Lippman, Lippman referred to both Laing and Thomas Szasz, and concluded that "mad" does not really mean anything anyway (KMM 25 BHP 16, October 30, 1974). Again, in late 1974, Head herself—perhaps referring to Wood and Lippman—wrote to Carol Mhene that "alarmed outsiders say I need Laing to analyse me" (KMM 50 BHP 8, November 17, referring to *A Question of Power*). Finally, in 1977, she wrote to Betty Fradkin describing the "frightening alarm and originality of R. D. Laing" (KMM 15 BHP 45, April 3, 1977). OK, so Head was familiar with Laing's ideas.[3]

It turns out she was also familiar with the anthropologist Ruth Benedict's book *Patterns of Culture*. In "Notes for Seminar – WHAT DOES THE

---

3  In a letter of October 30, 1978, to Verna Hunt, Head wrote that she had two copies of Laing's *The Politics of Experience* and said, "I was trying to say the same thing in 'A Question of Power'" (KMM 123 BHP 6), that the individual lives multiple lives.

BOTSWANA NOVEL SAY" (KMM 457 BHP 28), she wrote on page 3 that "I accept as valid the proposition made by an American anthropologist, Ruth Benedict, that the roots of racial prejudice and nationalism go deep," and quoted *Patterns of Culture* at length, arguing that a novel can be both national and international at the same time. (I will consider this point in more detail later, in chapter 4; right now I want to focus on Laing, Foucault, and Head.) What I was discovering, in fact, was an affinity in Bessie Head with the ideas of Laing and Benedict. I think that there is also an affinity (albeit limited) for Michel Foucault. In particular, the ideas of Laing and Foucault about the nature of individual psychological existence, the way societies develop moral and other codes according to what is important to them, and the way that European society in particular has used language and science to control socially aberrant individuals echoes strongly with what Bessie Head describes in her work. This discussion is interesting, but of course, since Bessie Head is always open-ended and unresolved, these thinkers are ultimately inadequate. But I still think they illuminate some very important aspects of Bessie Head's trilogy. And so I will look at them again, briefly.

Laing was concerned most specifically with the nature of schizophrenia[4] and with how people develop multiple facets of their personalities in order to deal with different social situations and pressures. Laing suggested that schizophrenics fear a loss of identity, and they perceive that loss as possibly happening in one of two ways: either their own identity is engulfed by the identity of other(s) (*The Divided Self* 44), or they feel themselves so empty that it is in danger of imploding under pressure from the outside "reality" (*The Divided Self* 45). The first experience, of engulfment, would apply to both Margaret of *Maru* and Elizabeth of *A Question of Power*: Margaret finds her mind invaded by dreams from Maru, and Elizabeth's mind is occupied for long periods by Sello, Medusa, and then Dan. Laing believed that schizophrenics can recognize both alienation and what he called social fantasy, shared "structures of experience" that "come to be experienced as objective entities"

---

4 It is important to note how Laing approached mental illness. Laing, as an early influence in the anti-psychiatry movement (along with Michel Foucault), believed that common psychiatric treatments of the time were damaging to patients, and that medical concepts were inappropriately applied to mental and emotional conditions that were shaped by social factors.

(*The Politics of Experience* 77). We observe it as social and behavioral norms, customs, rituals, manners, and so on. In Laing's model, all groups operate by social fantasy (*Self and Others* 39); thus a society's history and culture illustrate either the successful participation in fantasy by the members (through rites, taboos, holy days, etc.) or the successful imposition by some of a particular fantasy (for example racial or sexual subordination) on all the other members. Adapting to a social fantasy, playing a role in that fantasy, alienates people from their own experiences and therefore from their own selves. In other words, for Laing, social roles might be the problem, as in fact they were for Head herself, who wasn't an ethnic Motswana and didn't play by those rules. But for Bessie Head's characters, as I will discuss later, they offer a solution.

Laing's work addresses two aspects of madness: as a response to alienating social circumstances, but also as an expression of a deeper understanding of the human condition, the potential of knowing the absolute truth about human existence in oneself. Here we come to Foucault and to the idea of the wise madman who is in a way blessed and who can see things others cannot. In *The Politics of Experience*, in fact, Laing described this second aspect as a kind of journey, but his journey is an almost self-indulgent luxury of intellectual and emotional illumination. This kind of self-indulgence acknowledges neither the pain of real mental illness nor the terror of Elizabeth's battles with Sello, Dan, and Medusa.

Still, Bessie Head recognized the challenge of that absolute truth: "But between two living human beings there is always Truth and Truth is like that double-edged thing and is constantly expressing itself as Fireworks" ("God and the Underdog" 46). For Head, those fireworks are an honest representation of human experience; they can be awkward, uncomfortable, and even painful, but they are necessary, perhaps inevitable. Like Laing, Head seemed to believe that the truth of the self is knowable.

The philosophy and writing of Michel Foucault would suggest the same thing: Foucault and Head both objected to the way that theories and ideologies are used to establish a norm for human behavior that pathologizes, criminalizes, or ignores any variation.[5] In *Madness and Civilization: A History of Insanity*

---

5  Mark Philip, in a discussion of Foucault's general ideas on confinement, noted that Foucault is often criticized for offering a new theoretical approach, but he believes that Foucault "would deny

*in the Age of Reason*, Foucault examines the history of how attitudes towards madness in Europe and the rise of mental institutions can be understood as evidence of the imposition of social control. In the preface, he outlined what he thought was the essential problem of confinement of the mad: "[T]he man of madness communicates with society only by the intermediary of an equally abstract reason which is order, physical and moral constraint, the anonymous pressure of the group, the requirements of conformity" (x). That conformity ignores something important: "In the Middle Ages and until the Renaissance, man's dispute with madness was a dramatic debate in which he confronted the secret powers of the world; the experience of madness was clouded by images of the Fall and the Will of God, of the Beast and the Metamorphosis, and of all the marvelous secrets of Knowledge" (xii). Foucault traced attitudes to the phenomenon of madness, from the decline of the early medieval Ship of Fools (*Narrenschiff*) to the belief that madness (or folly) gets to the heart of reason and truth, to Baroque representations of animality ("it is animality that reveals the dark rage, the sterile madness that lie in men's hearts" [21]), to the idea that madness exists in every man as a sign of his own self-attachment (narcissism), and finally, "to the moral world, [where] also belongs the *madness of just punishment*" (30), that is, work.

Ultimately, madness embodied the evil represented by the absence of morality. Foucault, in the preface, laments that the introduction of the moral aspect has erased the "exchange between madness and reason" (x) and suggests that madness expresses something important: it is "A realm . . . where what is in question is the *limits* rather than the *identity* of a culture" (xi, my emphasis). Madness thus can define the boundaries of possible human existence, of possible human knowledge, and it has value because in the personal moral structure of the madman, it reveals other possibilities. Madness here is romanticized and useful. In Bessie Head, madness, although perhaps necessary, is certainly not romanticized.

---

that he is offering a new theory of social and political order because, above all, his concern is with the destruction of such theories" (69). Philip thinks that Foucault conveniently (and, I would add, disingenuously) ignores this criticism. I believe that Bessie Head is also interested in the destruction of ideology but that, unlike Foucault, she faces the contradictions head-on.

In the introduction to her study of the language of madness in Bessie Head and Janet Frame, Susanna Zinato wrote that "true madness cannot be told" (21); in other words, "writing" madness is artificial; it imposes an order that is absent from true psychosis. Literary madness must be constructed and is therefore not organic or "real." What this statement means for Bessie Head is that in *A Question of Power*, madness is both real and made up for some other purpose.

In her writing, Bessie Head insists not only on the validity of the personal moral structure but also on the importance of personal moral responsibility:

> I don't go along with any God who has the power to remove the sins of the world. I only accept that each soul is responsible for its own actions and that all souls, whether God or the devil walk the razor's edge of good and evil, that the pure and noble of today may be the demons of to-morrow. I throw the accent heavily on self-responsibility. (KMM 38 BHP 25, May 1, 1970, to Tom Carvlin)

This aspect appears to be absent from Foucault's "archaeology" of madness. Focusing on the importance of social structure in silencing and controlling madness means overlooking the equal importance of individual action, which is necessary to Bessie Head—in the idea of man as God and in the transient and corruptible nature of social moral structure. This complete inward-turning of Elizabeth's madness, the way it examines in detail not only every aspect of social conditioning but also of personal inadequacy, raises serious questions and difficulties for the reader—both literary, in Zinato's sense of the madness as artificial, and personal: "You are quite right. It is not a work of the imagination but a real experience" (KMM 6 BHP 4, June 12, 1974, to Christine Qunta). In Mandow's analysis, it means being implicated in everything that happens, as both victim and oppressor, a concept Head herself acknowledged when she wrote "I could be evil too" ("Some Notes on Novel Writing" 63).

Finally, Foucault's French, *fou*, does not appear to distinguish between a mad*man* and a mad*woman*.[6] This distinction, however, is important in

---

6 The French word for madwoman is *folle*, but Foucault does not appear to distinguish between them in *Histoire de la folie a l'age classique*. Many thanks to Dr. Sara Zumbika-van Hoeymissen for checking this for me.

English, particularly in feminist criticism and fiction and most notably in Sandra Gilbert's and Susan Gubar's *The Madwoman in the Attic* and Charlotte Perkins Gilman's *The Yellow Wallpaper* (the protagonist of which, along with Charlotte Brontë's Bertha Rochester in *Jane Eyre*, is the madwoman in the attic). Neither does Bessie Head distinguish between them in her philosophy of the brotherhood of *man*. A central tenet of feminist scholarship (in most disciplines) identifies this semantic issue as crucial to understanding patriarchal control of women. I think that this is an important concept, but I am also certain that, at least for me, it is irrelevant for reading and understanding Bessie Head. She "objects to being called a woman writer . . . 'Too many people have asked, "Are you a feminist?" ' " (KMM 392 BHP 2, "Bessie Head, Africa Centre," notes from a talk at the Africa Centre, London, May 16, 1980). She is "afraid you feminists *flatten* me with your causes. I am a storyteller by birth" (KMM 41 BHP 11, October 3, 1981, to Gloria Joseph, my emphasis). She insists that

> [a]ll the mad, wild feminists of the world passionately love A Question of Power and Elizabeth but they make a mistake. Elizabeth is brutally assaulted but she remains in close intellectual communication with the two men, particularly Sello, and heeds their communication because it is important. Elizabeth is a hugely integrated personality absorbing all her past lives, many of which could have been male, celibate and monk. They make a mistake. Elizabeth is not women. (KMM 74 BHP 117, July 27, 1983, to Paddy Kitchen)

In such feminist theoretical models as those of Gilbert and Gubar, moral failure is perceived to be always possible and even imminent in women because of the pathologization of femininity itself; because they are never really well in the same way that men are, they cannot be trusted to make sound judgements. Postcolonial criticism identifies a parallel pathologization of the Other, and postcolonial readings of *A Question of Power* in particular have looked at the many ways in which Elizabeth's madness is thus a consequence of racial injustice and gender oppression. Helen Kapstein, to take but one example, reads the madness of Elizabeth as a rhetorical strategy. In her analysis, madness exists on the border (however the border is defined—mentally, physically, geographically, etc.), and the "trespasser is mad" (72). For Bessie Head, however, these distinctions are irrelevant because all people have this dual nature (man/woman, self/other, good/evil) within themselves;[7] dealing with it and with the problems that it creates is what all three novels of the trilogy are about, and perhaps what we her readers have to learn is how to be honest with ourselves about it so that we can deal with other human beings honestly and fairly.

In "The Universality of Madness," Jacqueline Rose wrote that a major difficulty of reading *A Question of Power* is that the reader is "stuck" inside Elizabeth's head (403–4), an observation that Sarah Mandow elaborates on. *A Question of Power* moves from personal to historical to universal, but historical and universal are not antagonistic, and the movement not unidirectional (411). Anyone can speak in a racist voice, and in Bessie Head, anyone does.[8] What happens for the reader is that universality is paradoxically a "part" of interiority (416–17). Prejudice, injustice, and so on, do not only exist in one system; they exist in all systems, and therefore in us, and once again the reader is implicated as both victim and victimizer. In Bessie Head, there is no escape (it is "writing by battery assault" [Rose 404]).

In *A Question of Power*, madness is real and must be taken seriously because it is both a quest for self-knowledge and real, lived experience. For Head, and in her writing, institutionalization is not the easy answer: she described her own incarceration in the psychiatric hospital in Lobatse and noted that when she arrived, she was put in a cell with two women who had been condemned to hang for the *muti* murder[9] of young girls (KMM 51 BHP 6, January 28, 1973, to Dot Ewan).[10] In *A Question of Power*, Elizabeth is

---

7 This kind of duality is also characteristic of Jung's formulation of the different aspects of human psychic existence, especially in the archetypes of our collective unconscious and the shadow complex of our personal unconsciousness. There is a great deal more to be written about the Jungian aspects of Bessie Head's work.

8 As an aside, Rose wrote that "[t]his gives the postmodern shibboleth of flexibility and mobility its most sinister connotation" (412). See also Sue J. Kim, "'The Real White Man Is Waiting for Me': Ideology and Morality in Bessie Head's *A Question of Power*" (especially pages 49–55), for a discussion of how postmodernity, as characterized by Dan's torture of Elizabeth and by the confused nature of Elizabeth's "real" life during her struggle with Dan, contributes to Elizabeth's alienation.

9 Ritual murder for body parts to be used for making strengthing medicine. Two women were condemned for "child murder" at the time of Bessie's hospitalization. They were sentenced in April 1971 and executed in February 1972.

10 This strikes me as a frighteningly logical conclusion to Foucault's study of and thinking about confinement: at some point, if people who don't fit in will all face confinement of some sort, then why separate them at all from each other? People who are perhaps ill but harmless could very easily (and cheaply) be confined with those who are are dangerous.

treated by a doctor she characterizes as "stark raving mad too" (184) because of his own racism. The problems that Bessie Head wrote about, and the ideas referred to in the preceding discussion, are not simply abstract creations of "fevered minds."

*Not Either an Experimental Doll,* the correspondence between a young Xhosa girl and a woman who was attempting to be her benefactress, offers a real-life example of Laing's "social fantasy" as well as of Head's fireworks between two human beings. In her introduction to the correspondence, Shula Marks wrote that the letters "reveal the separate worlds which we all inhabit, but which are made more frightening and more separate by the divisions of age, ethnicity and race," and that in them "we see the overarching constraints of social structure on human agency, and the complex relationship of individual psychology with a culture-bounded social order" (1). Of course, every social order is culture-bound, and Lily Moya was trapped as much by her own expectations as she was by Mabel Palmer's.

Lily Moya was a young Xhosa schoolgirl, and Mabel Palmer was an English woman retired from her position at the University of Natal. Lily's requests for financial and subsequently emotional assistance demonstrate her desire to leave the constricting circumstances of the life that was expected of her. The letters show two women, both persistent and ambitious, but who have little understanding of how the other lives. Their failure to come to an understanding in spite of their determination to develop some kind of relationship demonstrates the difficulty of crossing the cultural boundaries between age, ethnicity, and race to which Marks refers. Mabel's inability to understand Lily's difficulties at school, where she was so different (younger, female, a Xhosa among Zulus), and Lily's expanding and insistent demands on Mabel's generosity paint a dismal picture for the possibility of bridging those boundaries. Mabel was very willing to help, but her plans for Lily did not correspond to Lily's own plans for herself. Lily transferred from one school to another in an attempt to find a place where she could fit in and succeed, but eventually Mabel's patience and ability to provide financial assistance ran out (183). Lily gave up trying to get an education and abandoned her friendship with Mabel: "Your letter has been handed to me. For congenial reasons I had to leave Adams, due to the fact that I was never meant to be a stone but a human being with feelings, not either an experimental doll" (185–86).[11] When Lily appeared at her family's home in Sophiatown after her failed attempts at school, "she was clearly in a disturbed state" (Marks 198). Marks notes that in interviews, Lily drew a clear link between her experiences in boarding school and her experiences in psychiatric hospitals: " 'My life was a transfer' " and " 'Mrs Palmer gave me scholarship to Sterkfontein' [psychiatric hospital]" (209).

Bessie Head's descriptions of Elizabeth's emotional difficulties in *A Question of Power* are reminiscent of how Lily understood her own life. True, or "real" madness, like fictional madness, can be a complex expression of human experience, for example, in the way Lily identifies her "scholarship." Like Lily, Elizabeth responds to her present circumstances in terms of her background, but Elizabeth's triumph lies in her ability to move into her future (an option that did not exist for Lily). And literary madness can allude to an aspect of total human life, one that often can clarify and interpret lived experience. The history of madmen in literature is crowded with jesters, fools, and others who spoke the truth of the human condition (Foucault also briefly examines the wisdom of the fool or the madman); certainly *A Question of Power* has been read this way.

One such example can be found in Roger Berger's "The Politics of Madness in Bessie Head's *A Question of Power*." Berger asserts that Elizabeth "conquers the psychopathology of the colonial encounter" (42). He discusses Elizabeth's madness as a function of the colonial encounter and suggests that Head's text "offers an intriguing extension of Fanon's paradigm" (41) for the liberation of all humankind because Elizabeth experiences oppression in both a colonial and a neocolonial world. She finds her "cure" in a return to a "global human vision" (39) which echoes Fanon's affirmations of humanity in *Black Skin, White Masks*: "No attempt must be made to encase man, for it is his destiny to be set free" (230). Apparently, we are to believe that madness makes you free.

When I wrote my original dissertation, this is the point at which I began: madness as revelatory of something important about the human

---

11 This quotation has eerie echoes with *Maru*, in which Margaret Cadmore Junior becomes the material for Margaret Cadmore Senior's experiment: "As she put the child to bed that night in her own home, her face was aglow. She had a real, living object for her experiment. Who knew what wonder would be created?" (230).

experience. I was struck by the way most modern psychotherapy (as opposed to psychiatry), as I saw it represented at that time, seemed to involve helping sick patients adjust to the demands of their lives. I considered the possibility that people spent countless millions each year visiting therapists who promised to work with them in overcoming phobias, learning to get along with others, and achieving success in their workplaces, whereas we seldom seemed to question whether the demands were unreasonable, whether the phobias stemmed from real dangers, whether others *were* difficult to get along with, or whether workplaces were not designed for our success.

I have a different perspective on these things now, partly because I live here, in Botswana, as an outsider, like Bessie herself, and partly because, also like Bessie, I am more willing to recognize my own role in making my life, which has brought me here to Botswana. In 1996 I wrote, "Sometimes, even when we recognize the structural flaws in our lives, we are reluctant to acknowledge that alleviating the problem might not be a question of changing something— some behavior—in ourselves." That statement now seems very naive. People are sometimes sick, and modern medicines can alleviate much suffering that earlier was simply shoved under the ancestral carpet or dismissed as a result of stress. I do not discount the importance of disease and organic malfunction in the human being, nor do I propose in any way that all madness has a social cause. My project is not psychotherapeutic or psychiatric but literary and personal: I want to know why reading Bessie Head has the effect on me and other readers that it does. Laing and Foucault gave me places to start, but in the end, the experience can only come from ourselves.

Of course, social institutions often appear monolithic, immutable, permanent, and eternal, perhaps because they rely on constructions of normality provided by unassailable science (Foucault), whereas we view ourselves as flexible and amenable to change, making it our job to change ourselves. Head herself recognized the power of social institutions, but she also understood that social institutions are not immutable and permanent. Her physical and social circumstances—single mother, poor, an exile, then a citizen who did not speak the same languages as other citizens, someone who was often the victim of vicious gossip, but also someone whose behavior was often incomprehensible to her neighbors—impacted absolutely everything she did.

In 1993 Mary Kay Blakely wrote about a problem she called "political depression," the kind of depression people experience when they face a world over which they have no control.[12] I am struck now by the obvious relevance of this problem for Bessie Head, who was less well equipped than the usual village-dweller to face a society that was full of deep and hidden currents of manipulation and power struggles. Eilersen notes examples of Head being the victim of malicious rumors and so on. In one case, Head was supposed to have had a secret lover who was giving her money; this lover had also made her pregnant and Head was said to have killed the baby and thrown it down a pit latrine[13] (*Thunder behind Her Ears* 128). These threats were not imagined, and the whispering and the consequences of covert ostracization are still very real for very many: the closeness and intimacy of village life that are celebrated by some also mean isolation for others; these are real components of village life anywhere. Blakely suggested that we should not necessarily be trying to find ways to cope with and manage it: "To address the craziness itself . . . means raising threatening questions about our families, jobs, relationships, our whole society. Easier by far, if only temporarily effective, is to learn a few deep-breathing exercises" (28). Her conclusion gets to the heart of Foucault's analysis: the role that power and its institutions play in keeping people under control. Bessie Head insisted on the equal importance of individual responsibility. Deep breathing keeps us from challenging power relationships.[14] The power of Bessie Head's writing is that she acknowledges both how we are made to believe that there is something wrong with us and also that in fact we are responsible for our own lives.

Twenty-five years ago, in 1993, Blakely wrote that Americans

---

12 In 2017, more and more people seem to be suffering from this condition, but there are also signs that they know the external causes and their own role in solving the problems. Donald Trump, Bernie Sanders, Rodrigo Duterte, Brexit, Iceland's refusal to repay offshore pension money to Britain in the recession of 2008, Greek protests against the imposition of austerity measures, Black Lives Matter, Catalonia's bid for independence, Harvey Weinstein's downfall: all these contradictory figures and crises point to a strong undercurrent of desire on the part of ordinary people to take back their power as citizens and destroy the status quo.

13 Such forms of infanticide were not uncommon.

14 George Bernard Shaw: "The reasonable man adapts himself to the world; the unreasonable one persists in trying to adapt the world to himself. Therefore all progress depends on the unreasonable man" (*Maxims for Revolutionists* #124, 1903).

are one nation of split realities: One fact in the newspaper—the 200,000 episodes of televised violence, let's say—has one meaning for Arnold Schwarzenegger, an actor with made-up wounds in fake wars who supports real military aggression, and another for someone like Eddie the Loop, a dismembered veteran from a real war who now leads an unimaginable life under a Manhattan bridge. Whose reality is the authentic one? Either some of us are crazy, or there is no such thing as "the real world." Or there is, but as the late physicist Frank Oppenheimer once said, "We don't live in the real world. We live in a world we made up." (28)

Or, conversely, and paraphrasing Dumbledore, what goes on in our heads might also be very real.

3

# "They Also Forgot He Was a Man"

*Possibly two thirds of the nation are still women and about children*
*procreated under such circumstances, the men hardly seem to care.*
"Despite Broken Bondage, Botswana Women Are Still Unloved" 57

*That kind of man lived near the animal level and behaved just the same.*
*Like the dogs and bulls and donkeys, he also accepted no responsibility*
*for the young he procreated.*
"The Collector of Treasures" 91

*I think that African women, more than women anywhere else in*
*the world, have a long traditional history of oppression. One finds*
*all sorts of sayings in traditional culture that relegate to women an*
*inferior position in the society such as: "A woman is sacred only if she*
*knows her place which is in her yard, as a mother of children and a*
*housewife." A number of oppressive traditions completely obliterated*
*her as a thinking, feeling human being, so that even until today this*
*stigma lingers. I have been told by a black man that most African men*
*will shy away from an educated, intellectual African woman with the*
*observation: "We don't want two men in the house." A thinking, feeling*
*woman is a real threat and makes the men feel insecure.*
"Societal Values and Women: Images vs. Real Life" 47–48

There is no doubt that Bessie Head understood the situation of women
in Botswana society and thought deeply about the problems they faced (and
continue to face) and how these problems came into existence.[1] She wrote to
Tony Hall (February 24, 1979),

---

1 The stories in *The Collector of Treasures* deal almost entirely with women in situations of rural
poverty, migrant labor and family breakdown, traditional Tswana attitudes towards women and
their place in society, and so on, and are often cited in this context.

I feel the new age belongs to those who serve life. Women's lib. for me tends to fall into this broad category. The independence of women is certainly a needed thing; it overcomes problems of prostitution and if a woman is independent financially it gives her time to find out if she really loves a man and is not merely dependent on him for support. (KMM 47 BHP 42)

There is also no doubt that Bessie Head did not consider herself a feminist, because she hated the "form of ruthless feminism that excludes men" that she saw, for example, in *Ms.* magazine and did not "swallow all the Ms propaganda, against men and men. I just like men. I like women too. But I don't like things to be unbalanced like that" (KMM 15 BHP 17, October 26, 1975, to Betty Fradkin). And she continued in her letter to Tony Hall, above, that "[t]here is something shrill there that I do not like. Some women push to totally eliminate men from the scheme of things" (KMM 47 BHP 42). For Bessie Head, the issue was always one of "political camps" that "falsify truths" and abuse power; anyone, male or female, could abuse power.

I was in high school around this time, in the mid-1970s. I had a dreadful sense, despite the fact that my parents never pressured me, that I was going to have to get married and have children, but I was nowhere near ready, nor was I sure I wanted that life. I had been raised by a stay-at-home mother, and had passed through a quite happy childhood, in large part because I knew my mother was always home (she did not go back to work until later) and because my father spent nearly all his non-working hours with us, his family. But when I got to high school, I changed—and probably the rest of my family did, too, although I would not have seen it, being a teenager and all. I was miserable in high school: I did not fit in with any of the usual groups, and my classes were boring. I wanted to be a writer, a pianist, a foreign correspondent, but all I could see for myself was the life my mother had. My mother had no regrets; she made that abundantly clear to us. My parents simply expected us to get educated and do what made us happy, but everywhere else I turned I could only see wifehood and motherhood, and I was often filled with dread.

Then I discovered *Ms.* magazine. The first issue came out in December 1971, the year before I started high school. In its pages, I found women writing about my life and my anxieties. I began to wonder if the life I saw was indeed inevitable. It took me about ten years to realize that it wasn't, but I started to look for things that I could do before that other life happened to me. Finally, when I was about twenty-three, having studied in Germany for a year, having tried out different majors, graduating with the prospect of a scholarship to do a year of graduate study in West Berlin, a scholarship that guaranteed me a place in a graduate program, I finally realized that my life was my own. But until I made that discovery, I was miserable—and I probably made everyone else around me miserable, too.

As I got older, I thought a lot about my mother's life, the sacrifices she made and her own desire for the life she had—and her happiness in that life. And then, in 1989, as I started to work on Bessie Head, I began to see something else, something that both my parents had been teaching me my whole life. I also began to examine my own unquestioning allegiance to feminism. I had to. My allegiance had caused me to lose respect for the choices my mother had made and to ignore the sacrifices that both she and my father had made in order that I would have so many more choices.

When Head was writing in the 1960s and 1970s, the second wave of feminism was rushing over in Western society. The terms "feminism" and "women's liberation" had been around since approximately the turn of the century, when the first flowering of feminism focused on issues of political rights and enfranchisement: the word "feminism" came from a French term for the ideology that espoused the political equality of women in the nineteenth century. In the 1960s, "women's lib" was being associated not only with political feminism but also with other, more grassroots, movements for social equality, and articulation of that goal became formalized in forms of feminist theory that, by the 1980s, were being discussed in academia. But many felt that this more mainstream form of feminism overlooked other forms of women's oppression: lesbians, women of color, and working-class women began to argue for other viewpoints and a more varied understanding of the forms of oppression that women all over the world faced. The "shrillness" that Bessie Head heard in the cries for equality from for example *Ms.* magazine was expressed in the splintering of feminism into different "feminisms" in the 1980s, including Alice Walker's reformulation of the idea of womanism, which was first noted in the early 1980s.[2] This splintering is today viewed by some feminist theorists as a necessary and not at all threatening development, since feminism and the theorization of it is sometimes seen as particularly robust and receptive to criticism.

This splintering, however, had not yet widely occurred, and while Bessie Head clearly recognized that women, in particular women in Botswana, were getting the short end of the stick, she was put off by the idea that some people felt left out. Feminism, women's lib, turned out to be just another ideology, with all the problems that all ideologies drag in their wake. One group of people wresting power from another did not solve the fundamental problem of power and its consequences for everybody. Bessie Head was interested in the life of the soul and worked to transcend the physical through her writing, and so for her, "a man" and "a woman" are the same thing, and they both belong to "man." It seems pointless to me now to argue about it. She was both a product of her time and an independent thinker, who chose her words carefully. She meant words to mean the way she used them, but neither did she buy into anti-feminist discourse. Anti-feminist ideology, like feminist ideology, like any ideology, was dangerous.

This idea was a revelation to me, and it is one I still grapple with. Bessie Head's thought is not dependent on distinctions of masculine and feminine in many of the ways that we understand them, either within feminism or outside of it. So when I began work on rewriting this chapter, it became clear that a different concept must be at work in Head's thought. For Head, "gender" was not an concept, social or otherwise. People did what they needed to do, and men were biologically male, women biologically female. What they did with their biologies did not really matter. Men could be good or bad, as could women—but why? I revisited the stories in *The Collector of Treasures*, a text often lauded as Head's most feminist, and there was Paul Thebolo, assuring Dikeledi, as she was hauled off to prison, that he would care for her children. This was a clue, right in front of me the whole time.

2  It is not clear if Head knew of Alice Walker's reformulation, which celebrates women's rights and achievements in all cultures, not just white culture, as "mainstream" feminism was perceived to do. Head exchanged letters with Walker but ended the correspondence in 1978, before Walker's first recorded use of the term.

So I decided that this chapter has to be about women as mothers, and mothers as parents, who could just as easily have been men, as fathers, as parents. I look at motherhood because mothers are more common in the trilogy than fathers: they are more common in part because Head herself was a mother, in part because she was attached to her foster mother, in part because she did not know who her father was, in part because she idealized her own biological mother, and in part because there were a lot of single mothers in her own community. She wrote about what she knew, but she extrapolated from that experience of parenthood to generalize from mothers to fathers, to all relationships between all people: "the brotherhood of man." For Bessie Head, to be a man or a woman is the same thing—a human being.

Although the quotations that open this chapter would seem to expose Head for the feminist she "really" is, I believe that in fact they reveal something else about her writing. Men fail because they do not take responsibility for their actions. Women fail for the same reasons. But, not surprisingly, "responsibility" includes more than just taking care of the children. Being a parent, in the case of these three novels being a mother, means taking care of the children and through them taking care of everything that touches your life. That was the choice my parents made. And until I started delving deeper into Bessie Head's other writing, it was also the choice that I sneered at.

* * *

On May 1, 1970, Head made an important statement in a letter to Tom Carvlin, a statement that for me characterizes her own inner struggle, her impatience with others, her recognition of the importance of independence for women, and her criticism of feminism and other ideologies. I've already quoted it once, but for me it bears repeating:

> I don't go along with any God who has the power to remove the sins of the world. I only accept that each soul is responsible for its own actions and that all souls, whether God or the devil walk the razor's edge of good and evil, that the pure and noble of today may be the demons of to-morrow. I throw the accent heavily on <u>self-responsibility</u>. (KMM 38 BHP 25)

Head's insistence on introspection and on being accountable for what one does delineates her thinking sharply from that of both Laing and Foucault. Their critiques focus almost entirely on the role of society in fostering "madness" in the individual by offering only limited opportunities for self-expression within the constraints of custom and belief. Laing and Foucault ignore self-determination and self-will and thus make it easy for their subjects to abdicate responsibility for their own actions and lives. In Bessie Head's world, you cannot escape what you have done and therefore what you have to do. In particular, in each of the three novels of the trilogy, caring for a child reveals something important about character and draws people together: Makhaya to Paulina through Paulina's children, Margaret Cadmore Senior to Margaret Cadmore Junior through the latter's mother, Elizabeth to the people of Motabeng through Shorty.

In "The Universality of Madness," Jacqueline Rose refers to Bessie Head's statement that "each individual, no matter what their present origin or background may be, is really the total embodiment of human history" ("Notes from a Quiet Backwater II" 77). Rose infers from this quotation that in *A Question of Power*, "the woman becomes the repository of an unspoken and unspeakable history" (410). But even in the quotation that Rose refers to, Head notes that *every* person is this repository. Sello wants Elizabeth to see her part in the suffering and salvation of mankind: "She had seen from the beginning that she had no distinct personality, apart from Sello" (32). Head also wrote that "Elizabeth is not <u>women</u>. The student . . . is WOMAN" (KMM 74 BHP 117, July 27, 1983, to Paddy Kitchen), making a careful distinction between the physical fact of biological femaleness, which is indisputable but irrelevant, and the impossibility of Elizabeth being some kind of "universal woman," representing the entire history and suffering of all womankind (since she, like all people, somehow contains all of *human* history). Instead Head emphasizes the intellectual intimacy among Elizabeth, Sello, and Dan, an intimacy that would seem to have little to do with their respective sexes and more to do with their personalities.

The horrors of apartheid also belong to everyone. Shortly before her first hospitalization, Elizabeth remembers when she lived in Cape Town. One man asked her,

> "How can a man be a man when he is called a boy? I can barely retain my own manhood. I was walking down the road the other day with my *girl*, and the Boer policeman said to me: 'Hey boy, where's your pass?' Am I a man

to my *girl* or a boy? Another man addresses me as boy. How do you think I feel?" (44, my emphasis)[3]

These experiences are not limited to men or women but belong to all people. Head affirms the general nature of abuse of power, rather than the sexist (or racist or even classist) abuse of it.

*A Question of Power* also challenges the premise of Elizabeth's mother's insanity. Both Roger Berger (36) and Adetokunbo Pearse (82) make the interesting observation that the reader cannot be sure, given the evidence in the text, that Elizabeth's mother actually was mad. As Head describes them, the mother's actions draw attention to the unreasonableness of what she did—having sexual relations with a black man—and therefore her behavior, rather than her psychology, is the focus of the madness. Because of her careful attention to her daughter's education, Berger believes that Elizabeth's mother was probably more hopeless than insane, given her subsequent suicide.[4] Like Margaret of *Maru*, who carries the burden of helping her people (231), Elizabeth carries the burden of her mother's presumed insanity: " 'Do you think I can bear the stigma of insanity alone? Share it with me' " (17). The importance of mothering as both a woman's role as well as a socially identifiable and socially sanctioned one provides an anchor for Elizabeth in her own suffering and salvation. Motherhood is central, but as a social concept it is not examined, in Bessie Head's novels, perhaps because it is just there, and is almost always the first relationship we have with another human being. Another, in Head's world, would be fatherhood.

Perhaps I was unable to see the centrality of these two relationships because they were an intrinsic part of my childhood. I have met many adults (including my own mother) whose childhoods were not cushioned by the kind of environment my parents provided for us. But in Bessie Head I was presented with male characters who were not "feminist" in the ideological sense, but who were very much like my own father.

---

3 In Southern African linguistic contexts, "boy" can also be a term of insult for a man who is not acting like a circumcised adult, and in contemporary contexts is sometimes used dismissively (along with "girl" for a woman) by Southern African men and women. To a Boer, however, a black man was always a boy. And apparently a woman is always a girl.
4 Berger here is displaying the tendency to psychoanalyze that Sarah Mandow identifies. See earlier chapters.

At the beginning of *When Rain Clouds Gather*, Makhaya Maseko escapes from South Africa over the barbed-wire fence into Botswana. The first two women he meets are a girl and her grandmother, who rents him a place to sleep but who also offers to "rent" her granddaughter (10–11). Despite this unsavory introduction to Botswana, Makhaya makes his way to Golema Mmidi and meets Maria, Paulina Sebeso, and Mma-Millipede. Maria takes care of her elderly father Dinorego and marries Gilbert, a white agricultural aid worker who has cast his lot with the inhabitants of Golema Mmidi. Mma-Millipede is the great friend of Dinorego and a very devout woman who helps Makhaya see his own humanity as well as the humanity of all, and Paulina Sebeso is a widow with two children who is looking for an equal partner rather than a one-night stand. Makhaya accepts Gilbert's offer to teach the women of the village how to grow tobacco, and finds himself, in spite of his own prejudices, drawn to Gilbert as well as to the life that is being created in the village.

In this novel, the protagonist is a man, and three women have central positions in the unfolding of the plot; women in general are portrayed as hardworking partners in ensuring the success of Golema Mmidi. The work that women do is assumed to be important, not just by Gilbert and Makhaya, but by the writer herself. The rhythms of their work are graceful and seem almost choreographed.[5] On the day of Maria's marriage to Gilbert, the women butcher the goats and prepare the marriage feast:

> Everyone had brought along a little something to put into the pot. Mostly it was potatoes, and these little gifts were tied up in gay blue, red and yellow checkered cloths and hung from the waists of the women, and these checkered splashes of colour swayed about as they talked. At a sign from Paulina, an abrupt and deathly silence fell on the gathering. A few women moved forward and sliced out the hard fat that had surrounded the intestines of the animals and which, when heated, melted down into oil. This fat was divided into equal portions and placed in two large iron pots which

5  I would like to acknowledge Prof. Modhumita Roy who, at a colloquium in Pietermaritzburg in July 2007, made this point during a discussion of her paper " 'Everyone Had a Place in My World': Bessie Head's Utopia in *When Rain Clouds Gather*" (*The Life and Work of Bessie Head* 255–68). This rhythm is also present in *A Question of Power*; see e.g. page 111, when Elizabeth and Kenosi, described as "a perfect work-team together," face the prospect of disruption with the arrival of Tom. Fortunately, Tom also "works beautifully."

stood near the fire. On top of this fat they poured small packets of curry powder. Another group of women advanced on the slaughtered goats and, within a short space of time, sliced away all the meat, leaving behind the bony skeleton. The meat, fat, and curry powder then boiled away in big pots. Everyone moved over to small wooden tables, on the top of each of which was placed a basin containing water; and then, with strained, absorbed faces, the women peeled the potatoes, tossing them one by one into the basins. Even the goats quietened down, absorbed in munching the peels with their small dainty mouths. (101)

The next day, the women begin taking lessons from Makhaya on growing tobacco. They meet in the yard of Paulina Sebeso, where they prepare morning tea for themselves:

As always, when women left their own homes for the day, they took with them their food supplies in the bright checkered cloths, and these they undid now. One of the women stood up and collected small helpings of tea-leaves and powdered milk from each bundle, and then both the powdered milk and tea-leaves were poured at the same time into the boiling water. By the time Paulina emerged, dressed and washed, with her small daughter, tea was ready and poured. Also a plate of flat, hard sorghum cakes was handed around. Paulina took a few of the cakes off the plate and wrapped them in a cloth and handed this to the child, instructing her, as it was school holidays, to go and spend the day at the home of Mma-Millipede. Then they all drank the tea with clouds of vapour rising up from the mugs into the cold air. Each woman then carefully rinsed her mug and tied it up once again in the checkered cloth. They arose and walked in a brisk, determined group to the farm, Paulina taking the lead as she always and automatically did. (117)

This rhythm is repeated in the work of building the first experimental tobacco sheds—when Makhaya discovers that Paulina's daughter Lorato is constructing a mud village[6] (121–26)—and of pounding the week's sorghum into meal (156–57). At the weekend, Makhaya arrives at Paulina's yard to help with the village, and while Paulina pounds the meal, Makhaya and Lorato prepare grass and trees for the miniature village, working "the whole afternoon

---

6  Children commonly build such villages in Botswana. Being an urban South African, Makhaya is probably encountering such a village for the first time.

on this in absorbed silence, like two children of the same age who took life very seriously. Paulina worked nearby in silence, too" (156–57). But when Makhaya goes over to her to make some tea, he watches her and "upset the accuracy with which she hurled the pestle into the stamping block" (157). All the work is described by Head the writer in terms of its rhythms and its importance.

Everyone's work is important and respected, and Lorato becomes the excuse for Makhaya to visit Paulina's yard: "He ignored Paulina Sebeso as carefully as he ignored all the women, but he also sat in her yard and drank wood smoke tea until the stars came out," because "Paulina Sebeso had a very pretty little girl who walked like a wind-blown leaf, and Makhaya was in a mood just then to like a little girl like that" (156). Through this work with Lorato on her model village, which he encounters through his work with the women of the tobacco cooperative, Makhaya begins to take on responsibility for others: the women, Lorato, then Paulina's son Isaac, who ought to be at school and not tending cattle, and then finally Paulina herself.

Paulina is strongly attracted to Makhaya because she senses the strength of his inner life. She herself is looking for a man to possess all to herself, because it seems to her that in her society, "all the excessive love-making was purposeless, aimless, just like tipping everything into an awful cess-pit where no one cared to take a second look. And Paulina was too proud a woman to be treated like a cess-pit" (125). The words "purposeless" and "aimless" are telling here, in part because they contradict the "intense," "absorbed" way in which important work is conducted. For Paulina, a physical and emotional relationship is too important to be treated so casually.

Paulina's determination to maintain her self-respect, and to insist that men do the same and take responsibility for their actions, is most evident when her son dies. Isaac has been left at the cattle post to look after Paulina's cattle. During the drought, he contracts tuberculosis, and his sister, who knows that he has a cough, wants to knit him a cap. The news disturbs Paulina, and she undoes Lorato's work so that she can make it more quickly (135). When the cattle begin to die in the drought, Isaac does not return home with the other cattlemen, and Paulina makes plans to go to the cattle post to fetch him. Later, Mma-Millipede worries that Paulina will kill herself out of guilt over his death, possibly out of a sense of failure to protect him.

However, Paulina's actions as mother of Lorato and Isaac do not receive much attention; mother-love can be a cliché, and Head does not let her readers walk down that path. Instead, she makes Makhaya's reactions more interesting. Isaac's death forces Makhaya to see his love for the mother, Paulina. Paulina's desire for a man who will love her and her alone, and who will love her as an equal, is met in Makhaya.

Early in their relationship, Makhaya admits to Gilbert that he is not so much running away as " 'trying to run into. I want a wife and children' " (30).[7] As he listens to Gilbert's plans for improving life in Golema Mmidi (Gilbert, who is "intent only on being of useful service to his fellow men" [88]), he considers that "he might be more proud to count up the number of his fellow men he had helped to live, rather than the number he had bombed into oblivion" (90). Makhaya, like Gilbert, feels a sense of responsibility towards other people.

Bessie Head is interested in this sense of responsibility, but she introduces it almost accidentally in *When Rain Clouds Gather*. She understood *When Rain Clouds Gather* as belonging at the beginning of her development as a writer[8] and compared Makhaya to Maru, on one occasion referring to "dithering Makhaya" (KMM 24 BHP 34, January 22, 1972, to Giles Gordon).[9] But Makhaya's thoughts about himself and what he wants—an ordinary life— are the first expressions of what Head will refer to in *A Question of Power* as the "brotherhood of man"—and Golema Mmidi is the first place where this "brotherhood" might be found. When Makhaya considers the very real possibility that Paulina's child will have died at the cattle post, and then decides to accompany her, he reveals an awareness of his obligations towards his own and others' well-being: "What sort of man was he who only gave way to love under extreme pressure and pain? . . . If he loved Paulina now and admitted it to himself, it was because he sensed that she might be facing tragedy, and that she could not face it alone" (178–79).

---

7  This is the choice my parents made and the one I rejected.
8  Head never commented on the manuscript for *The Cardinals*, which was only published posthumously.
9  See later in this chapter for her characterization of Maru in this context. I have never thought of Makhaya as dithering; I find him an extremely sympathetic character.

Surrounded by tragedy and seated in the shade of a ramshackle mud hut in the Botswana bush, he began to see himself. In retrospect he seemed a small-minded man. All his life he had wanted some kind of Utopia, and he had rejected in his mind and heart a world full of ailments and faults. He had run and run away from it, but now the time had come when he could run and hide no longer and would have to turn round and face all that he had run away from. Loving one woman had brought him to this realization: that it was only people who could bring the real rewards of living, that it was only people who give love and happiness.

As though to confirm his new trend of thought, he stirred a foot and found it brushed against a bundle of something, carefully tied up. He opened the bundle and in it was a collection of wood carvings, done by the small boy to occupy himself during the lonely hours of cattle herding . . . Makhaya looked at it for some time, struggling to capture a living image of a child he did not know. He hoped he and Paulina would never create a child who would be expected to carry burdens beyond his age. (185)

I have given these quotations at length because they address a number of the issues that are central to Head's thinking about the nature of human life, and about the nature of good and evil. Makhaya's "small-mindedness" comes from an impossible desire for some kind of utopia, the perfect world that is nowhere. Human life consists of "ailments and faults," more particularly the latter, not only idealized visions of love. Because he loves one particular woman, he is forced to face suffering, and he admits that he loves her in part *because* she faces suffering, and he wants to help her. He looks at and thinks about the carvings, and the human being who made them, and his next thought is about the child that he and Paulina will create—a child who will undoubtedly have to carry burdens, but not any "beyond his age."

But marriage is not necessarily the ideal institution to capture all these conflicting feelings. Marriage in *When Rain Clouds Gather* is presented in a number of conflicting ways. Mma-Millipede reminds Maria that if she had not married Gilbert, "'then not only would you have lost him, but we too'" (97), implying that marriage cements relationships in a society. Perhaps it does, and yet at the end of the marriage feast, Gilbert takes Maria by the hand and "together they walked away far into the bush" (115), alone.

That ambiguity becomes discomfort, even pain, in Head's next novel, *Maru*. The title character is a man with a vision and a duty given to him by "the gods who talked to him in his heart" (250) to make a statement about the racism practiced against the San[10] of Botswana. He manipulates the situation in Dilepe village so that his rival Moleka marries his sister Dikeledi and he himself finally marries Margaret and removes her from the village. When I first read *Maru*, I was enchanted by the story, by the characterization, and by the lyrical descriptions, but I was troubled by the ending, since despite the proclamations of coming freedom, it does not seem very happy for Margaret. It remains for me a very problematic work precisely because of how Maru makes his stand against racism—he marries Margaret, but takes her away—and because of how he treats Margaret. Maru *does* love Margaret, but his desire to manipulate her happiness makes his love as cruel as it is tender: his answer

---

10  Many debates take place about the correct terminology to use for the indigenous inhabitants of Southern Africa. Kuela Kiema writes about the complexity of naming in *Tears for My Land: A Social History of the Kua of the Central Kalahari Game Reserve, Tc'amnqoo*:

> Our oppression comes in different forms, and one of these is what we are called. We are known by many names, most of them imposed upon us by our oppressors. We are called San, Bushmen, Khoisan and/or Basarwa; however "Kua" will be the main term I use to refer to my people. Like the Bantu, we have many different tribal names and they refer to the different languages we use and the territories that we inhabit. (12)

> Before we begin this history, I will mention a few facts about the names of other groups. The majority of the people of Botswana are called Tswana, hence the name Botswana which means literally the country of the Tswana tribe. The plural for citizens of Botswana is Batswana, whereas one is called Motswana. The Tswana speaking tribes comprise eight so-called "main" groups: the Bangwato, Bakwena, Bangwaketse, Bakgatla, Batawana, Batlokwa, Barolong and Balete. The other Bantu people, such as Bakgalagadi, Bakalaka, Hambukushu, Wayei, Ovaherero, Batalaote, etc., make up the Bantu minority. In addition to these Bantu groups, you will also find us, the San, Bushmen, Basarwa, whom I will refer to as Kua in my dialect. The Bantu see us as their subjects and treat us that way.
>    Mistakes are made because many people, including researchers, do not realise that we identify ourselves differently according to whom we are speaking. If I meet a Tswana or Bantu, I say I am a Mosarwa, but if I meet a Naro or any other of my people I refer to myself as a Dcuikhoe. When speaking Setswana, I call myself a Mosarwa but when speaking English, I use the term Bushman or San. (14)

I have quoted Kiema at length because I would like to explain my use of the term "San" and to identify some of the complexities surrounding these naming issues. In *Maru*, Bessie Head used the term "Masarwa," which is derogatory and which she knew was derogatory, using it deliberately to provoke her readers (it is also gramatically incorrect, a fact which possibly annoys Setswana-speaking readers of the novel). The use of "Masarwa" was also fairly common among English-speakers at the time. The most important point is that there is no definitive "correct" use, and that the issue is far too complicated to go into here. I will use "San" because I am writing in English. Ideally, Margaret Cadmore Junior would be referred to by the name of her people, but that name is unknown, like the name of her mother.

to the question about what he would do if he discovers that she does not love him as much as he loves her is "Kill her" (317).

In addition, Margaret herself hardly speaks in the novel but is nearly always spoken to, or about. Her own desires simply do not matter, even to the enlightened Maru. In the letter in which Head describes Makhaya as "dithering," she also describes "the dubious Maru, painted up as a God and from there a more or less shaking but certain platform" (KMM 24 BHP 34, to Giles Gordon). Later in the same year she wrote to Betsy Stephens that although Moleka is not a well-developed character, "Maru certainly is . . . He is a God along the style of the Grecian myths" (KMM 77 BHP 3, June 16, 1972), ascribing to him both the power and duplicity characteristic of the ancient gods.[11]

Margaret herself is raised to think of herself as a kind of savior. She gets this sense of herself from the woman she refers to as her teacher, Margaret Cadmore Senior, sometimes referred to as Margaret's foster mother. The wife of a missionary, Margaret Senior is called to deal with a dead "Masarwa" woman and her newborn child. She decides to raise the child herself to prove one of her pet theories, "environment everything; heredity nothing" (230).[12] She ensures the proper burial of Margaret Junior's mother, but not before drawing a picture of her that she captions, "She looks like a goddess" (230).[13] Margaret Junior carries the picture with her, a link between the woman who gave birth to her and the one who raised her.

Margaret Senior, the teacher, functions as a surrogate mother, the only parent Margaret Junior knows; she receives not only her education but also her name from the teacher: "Her mind and heart were composed of a little bit of everything she had absorbed from Margaret Cadmore. It was hardly African or anything but something new and universal, a type of personality that would be unable to fit into a definition of something as narrow as tribe or race or nation" (230–31). But Margaret Senior makes sure that Margaret

---

11  When my husband was reading a draft of this chapter, he noted that "[t]hinking of him as a Greek god makes more sense of the story, in the way that the Greek gods played with mortals with an ultimate lack of real concern."

12  Margaret Senior here demonstrates her belief in the *tabula rasa* theory of development in human behavior, the belief that human beings are born with what we would now call a neurological "blank slate."

13  Head wrote to Randolph Vigne (in a mention of *Turbott Wolfe*), that "my mother in particular, in her soul, was a goddess" (*A Gesture of Belonging* 66, letter of November 14, 1968).

Junior knows who she is, and she reminds the child that " '[o]ne day, you will help your people' " (231). She also tells the child that " '[y]ou will have to live with your appearance for the rest of your life. There is nothing you can do to change it' " (233). At the same time that she creates this "universal" person, independent of heredity, she affirms a particular identity to the child: the picture, "your people," and "your appearance." Margaret Junior absorbs these lessons and accepts her vocation. In spite of everything, "the tin cans rattling" (233) and the verbal abuse, the lessons "kept the victim of the tin cans sane" (233). Margaret knows her purpose in life, but she simultaneously recognizes that she has very little control over her purpose. She is strong, but never shows her strength in her society because she has been socialized, including by Margaret Senior, to just accept what is given her.[14]

At the most critical moments of her life, Margaret must separate from a mother-figure. When she is born, her mother dies. When she graduates from teacher-training school and begins work, her teacher retires to England. Margaret Junior cannot imagine life without her teacher, but Margaret Senior sends her a tear-stained postcard from England, reminding her again of her responsibility towards the San: " 'I had to do it for the sake of your people. I did not want to leave you behind. Margaret Cadmore' " (235). Later, an analogous separation occurs when Maru takes her from her home to marry her: the Windscreen-wiper, a kid goat who with his mother has befriended Margaret, sees his mother slaughtered and flees to Margaret (325), who takes him along to her new home with Maru (329–30). Her identity and her purpose (and "burden" [231]) derive from an emotional affiliation to a woman she never knew and a social affiliation with a woman who is not her mother. She arrives in Dilepe with a strong sense of responsibility to "her people," but in Dilepe, she is unable to help them by any action of her own because their rights and status are simply not recognized.

When we meet Dikeledi, we find that she is also the sort of person who looks out for others:

---

14 Margaret Junior can be understood as a forerunner of Elizabeth, a kind of savior who is also acted upon.

[Dikeledi] drew in a sharp, hissing breath.

It was an instinctive, protective gesture towards the person sitting near her. Dikeledi had taken two slaves from her father's house and, without fuss or bother, paid them a regular monthly wage, and without fuss or bother, they dressed well, ate well and walked about the village with a quiet air of dignity. There was something Dikeledi called sham. It made people believe they were more important than the normal image of human kind. She had grown up surrounded by sham. Perhaps it was too embarrassing to see people make fools of themselves, because at one point she said: "I'll have none of that." (239)

Because of her sense of responsibility towards others, she takes Margaret under her wing and does not prove to be easy for Pete to handle when he tries to engineer Margaret's dismissal from the school.[15]

The marriages of Gilbert and Maria, Paulina and Makhaya, and Maru and Margaret have a certain element of social logic: Gilbert and Makhaya are outsiders, so that Maria and Paulina bring a social benefit by ensuring that the men will stay in Golema Mmidi. Maru's marriage to Margaret creates an opening for the San into mainstream society:

When people of the Masarwa tribe heard about Maru's marriage to one of their own, a door silently opened on the small, dark airless room in which their souls had been shut for a long time. The wind of freedom, which was blowing throughout the world for all people, turned and flowed into the room. As they breathed in the fresh, clear air their humanity awakened. (331)

Their marriage is socially logical, like the marriages in *When Rain Clouds Gather*, but it is also sterile, and that sterility makes the "solution" problematic. They do not remain in Dilepe or any other village where their union could give testimony to the value of all human lives. Instead, they live in a remote, isolated spot, exiled from everyone.

*A Question of Power* plunges most deeply into the nature of power and human responsibility. Isolation and exile are not possible for Elizabeth: she arrives into an established community with her young son. Elizabeth has to

---

15  Pete's character demonstrates his own class prejudices, since he apparently is reluctant to challenge Dikeledi, a member of the royal house, even though she is a woman.

navigate a complex path to understand her responsibility towards herself, her son, her community, and humankind.

What binds all these different aspects of life together is love. When Sello, the first of the three figures who come to Elizabeth, explains his appearance in her life, he introduces love by explaining the events that lead up to Elizabeth and to love: "'Everything was evil until I broke down and cried. It is when you cry, in the blackest hour of despair, that you stumble on a source of goodness. There were a few of us who cried like that. Then we said: "Send us perfection." They sent you. Then we asked: "What is perfection?" And they said: "Love."'" (34) Later, he explains that love is "two people mutually feeding one another" (197). Elizabeth's only connections to love are first her relationship to her imagined mother and second her relationship to her son.

Bessie Head herself created an image of her own mother that served her life as well as her storytelling. She imagined her mother as a brave woman: "I consider it the only honor South African officials ever did me—naming me after this unknown, lovely, and unpredictable woman" ("Preface to 'Witchcraft'" 72).[16] At school, she learned of "a pathetic letter written by my mother in the mental hospital, stipulating that above all things, it was her earnest desire that I receive an education and that some of her money should be set aside for my education" ("Notes from a Quiet Backwater I" 4). She held on to this image of her mother as a kind of spirit looking after her.

Elizabeth's mother did not display "proper" white femininity when she had sex with a black man, so it is no surprise that Medusa, the second figure to appear, exploits this "weakness" in Elizabeth. Although her taunts are as much racially charged as they are sexually charged, they are directed at Elizabeth as a woman. When Medusa imparts "some top secret information" about her vagina to Elizabeth, she says, "'You haven't got anything *near* that, have you?'" (44). She tells Elizabeth that she cannot survive in Africa because "'You're not linked up to the people'" (44); she will die like the "Coloured" men who "lay down on their backs" (45). "'That's what you are like,'" Medusa tells her, "'You

---

16 According to Eilersen, Bessie's own mother "insisted that the child be given her full name," Bessie Amelia Emery (*Thunder behind Her Ears* 9). Eilersen does not give a source for the mother's insistence.

have to die like them'" (45). Medusa mocks Elizabeth's biology, both in terms of her femininity and in terms of her not-black-not-white background.

Dan, the third figure to appear, persecutes Elizabeth for the same reasons: "You are supposed to feel jealous. You are inferior as a Coloured. You haven't got what that girl has got" (127). His nightly torture reflects his perception of Elizabeth's sexual—or feminine—inadequacies because she is not really African. Conversely, however, Dan is a stereotype of the oversexed African man who cannot be satisfied except by his Nice-Time girls: "he thrust black hands in front of her, black legs and a huge, towering black penis. The penis was always erected. From that night he kept his pants down; after all, the women of his harem totalled seventy-one" (128).

Essentially Dan wants to exercise power over Elizabeth by establishing for her a definition of what is appropriate and desirable, imposing and enforcing social standards of African femininity, as Laing and Foucault argued that society does. Dan demonstrates his power and her inadequacy by bringing the seventy-one Nice-Time Girls[17] into her room—even into her bed—and having sex with them. Dan is always careful to point out to Elizabeth why she cannot compare to them. She can never be respectable in Dan's eyes because she is neither a proper woman nor a proper African. He tells her, "'I go with all these women because you are inferior. You cannot make it up to my level because we are not made the same way'" (147); "'You have nothing. I've shown you all they have, but you have nothing'" (168). Such constant insults and confrontations predictably take their toll. But Dan's abuse is directed toward Elizabeth's outward appearance, not her inner life.

Elizabeth is confronted with an unrealistic model of femininity, one that is not her own. She and Margaret (of *Maru*) were raised in a society that rejected them at birth. Their rejection is categorical and absolute. There are no acceptable behavior patterns for them to follow, so they do not know where they fit in. Margaret simply succumbs to Maru's greater power, and Elizabeth becomes a nonentity, an impossibility, because there is no way for her to embody Dan's ideals. She cannot reconcile the ideals he parades through her room with her

---

17 The Nice-Time Girls are "a motley crew"; half of them are "goddesses" and half are "local girls" who are "supposed to be filled with power and sweet things they lacked and they were fillers for the time when his professionals were resting" (128).

own experiences in South Africa and Botswana. She is a woman, but she is not an acceptable one, not anywhere. She is a deviant, somewhat like Foucault's madman, who cannot be reached through the laws of human discourse.

Dan controls Elizabeth's sexuality by denigrating it; he asserts his own power by trying to make Elizabeth powerless, based on arguments about her physical self, rather than her soul, whereas Sello appeals to her soul. Elizabeth's very birth attests to the existence of female sexuality gone awry: her mother was not "controlled" in a socially acceptable way, and so she was incarcerated. If Dan can show her what "proper" African women are properly capable of, he can annihilate her sense of self-worth and self-esteem, and thus also control her. He nearly manages it, but, in his obsession with her sexuality, he overlooks one important aspect of her life.

For Elizabeth, being a mother is an advantage rather than a burden. That relationship saves her and helps make possible her reentry into human society. In Laing's model, social roles constrict the human spirit, but Elizabeth's role—her job—as Shorty's mother enables her to escape the nightmare of her other life. Shorty serves in a very basic way as a guide for his mother's interactions with the world outside her house. There are tasks he requires of her—whether he asks her or not—that anchor her to her other life: "He looked up at her trustingly. For all her haphazard ways and unpredictable temperament, she was the only authority he had in his life. The trust he showed, the way he quietly walked back to his own bed, feverishly swerved her mind away from killing him, then herself" (174). Even if Elizabeth "belongs" nowhere else, she belongs with her son. His role in her life is not central to the plot of the book, but his presence is assumed to be important: despite Elizabeth's insistence that she wants to be alone, she never can. The relationship between Elizabeth and her son receives more narrative attention than does the relationship between Paulina and her children in *When Rain Clouds Gather*, despite the importance of Isaac's death in furthering the relationship between Paulina and Makhaya. Shorty is always there and needs to be taken care of—food, sleep, medicine, and, in one very important instance, a football. (This is probably my favorite scene in the entire novel; people often assume that children bring chaos—and they do—but they also bring order and routine.)

On the day that Dan tells her to commit suicide, she wakes up to a mind that is completely empty:

> Shorty stood up and padded on bare feet to her bed. She couldn't remember his name. The cunning little bugger wanted his football. He smiled sweetly and rubbed her cheek. She was afraid to ask: "Who are you?"
>
> "You won't forget my football, mother?" he asked.
>
> The heavy weight of blankness shifted a little. So she was his mother, was she?
>
> "Yes," she said.
>
> "You must hurry up and make my breakfast," he said. "We get punished if we are late for school."
>
> "What's today?" she asked.
>
> "It's Friday," he said. "I know is Friday because yesterday we had library and library is Thursday."
>
> The heavy blanket shifted a little more. She hung on to his chatter about the football team. (193)

She is his mother; she must make his breakfast and buy him a football; he establishes the day for her by identifying temporal aspects of his own life. He places her in a context of affiliation.

Still, by twelve-thirty that day, her depression is so acute that she gets everything ready for her suicide at quarter to one. She never gets around to killing herself, though, because her son returns from school to play football, and she is distracted the whole afternoon watching him. The centrality of her son in her life—recognizing that she is responsible for him—keeps Elizabeth in a place where she forgets, literally, to kill herself. Her relationship to her son gives her back part of her being and makes her see how she is responsible for and to him, and also how she is responsible to other people. Significantly, after this episode, she remembers that she wanted to say something to Mrs. Jones, whom she had earlier slapped. She sends Shorty with a note of apology, and Mrs. Jones comes to visit Elizabeth immediately. Mrs. Jones tells her not to be afraid of evil because Jesus overcame it long ago (to which Sello agrees with a loud "Yes"), and then "Elizabeth stared back at her in disbelief. There was something on her face she had not seen for a long time; the normal, the human, the friendly soft kind glow about the eyes" (196). Not only is Shorty the physical intermediary for the note, but he is also the person through whom she comes back to her other self.

In Doris Lessing's *The Grass Is Singing* (a novel from an earlier decade and another place[18]), Mary Turner's perception of how to behave falls apart in a disturbing way: she acts out all the socially sanctioned roles, but in a socially offensive context, with Moses, her African houseboy. In her relationship with Moses, she exposes the structure of the institutions that at the same time prop her up. *The Grass Is Singing* reveals, in Mary's behavior, the absurdity of social norms, but it also reveals her part in the game. At her death, she feels remorse towards Moses, not Tony Marston, a representative of the white community who she thinks can help her. With Moses, she enacts the unspeakable: "it was the tone of Mary's voice when she spoke to the native that jarred on [Charlie]: she was speaking to him with exactly the same flirtatious coyness with which she had spoken to himself" (208). Finally, the images of the solitary lovers and the way that Head works out their place in a community offer a sharp contrast with the images of Moses and Mary at the end of Lessing's novel. In a perverse version of the walk that Head describes for Gilbert and Maria in *When Rain Clouds Gather*, Moses goes to stand beside an anthill to wait for the police to find him after he has killed Mary.

The consequences of Mary Turner's choices and actions bring no happy endings, no resolution. We are left to wonder if she did the right thing: "And, at the sight of [Moses], her emotions unexpectedly shifted, to create in her an extraordinary feeling of guilt; but towards him, to whom she had been disloyal, and at the bidding of the Englishman. She felt she had only to move forward, to explain, to appeal, and the terror would be dissolved" (243). Mary's sense of responsibility regarding her behavior towards Moses brings her to her death, making this relationship the only meaningful one she had.

However, Elizabeth finds deliverance in socially defined relationships, in particular as a parent, a mother. In the end, her life means facing her responsibilities: apologizing to Mrs. Jones, and—more importantly—taking

---

18  I love this novel for the way absurd social convention is made to look absurd. Other readers are very uncomfortable with the misogynistic idea that Mary Turner somehow got what she deserved. Tom Holzinger also noted (personal correspondence, October 21, 2012) that "in both Grass and Maru, the heroine is extinguished at the end of the novel, and in both cases with her full complicity."

responsibility for her son. In these kinds of actions, Elizabeth can learn and accept that she is connected to other people. Sello's concept of love as "mutually feeding one another" (197) takes concrete form in her relationship to Shorty and, subsequently, in her relationships to other people. Rather than just confining her, motherhood unites her to the very community that both gives her a sense of belonging and allows her to explore the experience of her own life. She finally becomes an adult woman, not merely a social one. Rather than suppressing her individuality, as both Laing and Foucault would appear to imply, the obligations of Elizabeth's social self enable her to find her personal self. In Setswana it is said that "*motho ke motho ka batho*," meaning that a person is only a person because of other people.

Jane Bryce-Okunlola discusses the importance of motherhood as an image central "to their concept of identity, continuity and creativity" (201) in the work of three African women writers, including Bessie Head. Bryce-Okunlola disputes the idea that the demands of motherhood are somehow incompatible with the demands of creativity, that is, that children somehow detract from or diminish a woman's creative process. She offers alternative readings of three writers whose works have often been interpreted to demonstrate that African women are "trapped" by motherhood;[19] she shows that instead they reconstruct it more accurately according to their own experience:

> For a writer, who by the very act of writing challenges the patriarchal appropriation of power over the Word, motherhood becomes a site of struggle . . . The writing of that desire by the author is a demonstration that, childless or husbandless, a woman *can* fulfil herself: through writing, the re-creation of her story in her own image, rather than that projected for her by her society. (201)

But for Elizabeth, and I think for Bessie Head too, motherhood is not a site of struggle. It is just there, because the child is there. Shorty does not represent the desire for something that is absent from Elizabeth's life; in fact, he is the means by which she can return to it.

---

19 One could consider, for example, Buchi Emecheta's *The Joys of Motherhood*, the title of which is clearly meant to be ironic, but which still critiques social perceptions of motherhood, not necessarily motherhood itself.

Mary Turner's desire for a child is certainly a longing for something, but the text demonstrates that it is a false longing, because what is absent from Mary Turner's life is Mary Turner herself.

> She thought of herself, as a child, and her mother; she began to understand how her mother had clung to her, using her as a safety-valve. She identified herself with her mother, clinging to her most passionately and pityingly after all these years, understanding now something of what she had really felt and suffered . . . she imagined her own child, a small daughter, comforting her as she had comforted her mother. (155)

Mary's desire repeats rather than rewrites her mother's experience, and therefore she is doomed to repeat her mother's life until she can take responsibility for her own actions. Mary spends her last day going through her life, first recognizing that something is wrong: " 'I have been ill for years,' she said tartly. 'Inside, somewhere. Inside. Not *ill*, you understand. Everything wrong, somewhere' " (238). Earlier in the day, she thinks about her life:

> For the evil was a thing she could feel: had she not lived with it for many years. How many? Long before she had ever come to the farm! . . . But what had she done? And what was it? What *had* she done? Nothing, of her own volition. Step by step, she had come to this, a woman without will, sitting on an old ruined sofa that smelled of dirt, waiting for the night to come that would finish her. (230)

She has done nothing "of her own volition," on her own responsibility.[20] At the very end, when "the terror engulfed her which she had known would come," when she is "in a trap, cornered and helpless," knowing that "she would have to go out and meet him" (241), only then is she overwhelmed by guilt towards Moses; only then does she understand.

Bryce-Okunlola's analysis of *A Question of Power* demonstrates the important place that Elizabeth's son has in her life, an importance, she notes, that is often glossed over or ignored completely by most critics. She wrote, "Just as Elizabeth's lack of a mother (mother-figure, mother-country, mother-tongue)

---

20  Lessing is possibly alluding as well to Jean-Paul Sartre's existentialist notion of "bad faith" (*mauvaise foi*), in which individuals have the freedom to act according to their own will, but succumb to societal forces and so act inauthentically.

is a major factor in her unsettled sense of identity, so is her own mother-role the route to her regeneration" (214). The concept of "mother" is a paradoxical one for Elizabeth: it defines her separation from any community in South Africa because of her own mother's transgression, but it also affirms the promise of a link between her and her new community in Botswana, in the form of her son. Elizabeth's relationship to her own mother forces Elizabeth to examine the power structures that put her mother in an asylum, and to think deeply and very personally about what such power structures, including her own role in them, have done to people throughout history. But her relationship to her son makes it possible to climb out of the cesspit of horror that is created by such power structures and to reconnect with people in a more meaningful way.

Towards the end of *A Question of Power*, when Shorty falls ill, Elizabeth goes out of her mind with worry: "On the Monday morning she jerked into life screaming in silent terror. Shorty had a high fever. Dan said he would be dead in two days' time . . . It was only a bruise on his knee that had festered and caused the fever. She . . . put him to bed and lay down. He fell fast asleep, with an Aspro" (197). When Dan tries to return to his activities with the Nice-Time Girls, Sello breaks the spell by telling her what love is, and "the words sank deep into her battered mind" (197). Her love for her son, the "normal" and "human," gives lie to Dan's cruelty and reveals his own recognition of the importance of the tie between parent and child—precisely in his effort to destroy it.

Similarly, Paulina and Makhaya are brought together through Paulina's worry about her own son Isaac and through the events of his death. Her terror regarding the fate of her son is eased somewhat by the fact that Makhaya's concern "lifted the weight off her arms and legs"; without even asking, he "had simply produced immediate solutions to her trouble" (173). When Paulina tries to get into the hut to see Isaac's body, Makhaya tells her, " 'Can't you see I'm here to bear all your burdens?' " (184). In the middle of the grief that he has chosen to share with Paulina, through his love for her, he decides that "He was just an ordinary man and he wanted to stay that way all his life" (194). Elizabeth knows that she is responsible for Shorty, but she does not realize immediately how central this relationship is for both of them. At the end of the novel, she finds a poem that he has written about their experiences: "She had to read it through several times in disbelief. It seemed impossible that he had really travelled the journey alongside her. He seemed to summarize all her observations" (205). He has, of course, been with her every step of the way.

In 1990, Carol Margaret Davison noted that "[s]uicide is, unfortunately, the most prevalent conclusion for women's novels of development" (23). But killing herself would be an abdication of all Elizabeth's responsibilities, and Head rejects that path for her. Instead, Elizabeth worries about Shorty and returns to the garden. Makhaya gives in to his love for Paulina as he takes on some of her burdens as his own. Margaret does not realize she has a choice; her identification as a "Masarwa" means that she is not strong enough to stand up to a chief, and so she follows Maru to a place removed from the society of others. Elizabeth's path is the only honest one—recognizing what you have done and taking responsibility for what you have done and what you can do (such as apologizing to Mrs. Jones for slapping her). This is not something only done by a mother, or a father: it must be done by everyone; being a parent is only one path towards what Head would call "real" true love.

As I have reread these novels with ideas about parenthood and about how responsibility toward, not freedom from, others brings true redemption, I have thought often of my own parents. Recently, when my sister asked me to write something for her Father's Day radio show, I remembered once when my dad came to my rescue.

I was nineteen and going to my first college party, a wine-and-cheese do at the community college I attended, just a few miles from our house. I was looking forward to the party because I was becoming giddy with increased independence. The party was held during my last semester there, before I went off to Germany to study for a year.

My father must have recognized the importance of this event for me, because when I telephoned him at two-thirty the next morning from a bowling alley about forty-five miles from home, needing to be fetched, he came immediately. My father never does anything immediately. (A few years later, when I had a late class downtown and had to be picked up at ten-thirty every Tuesday night from the empty bus station across from the really seedy bar filled with drunken leering men, he was invariably between twenty minutes and a half hour late. Invariably, he was sorry: "I was watching the game and lost track of time.") He must have been asleep when I called, and when he arrived, I apologized profusely. He said not to worry, that it was OK.

Shortly after my mother died in 2000, I spoke to one of her best friends, who told me that my mom was worried that she was not as "feminist" as I was. Oddly, as I was working on this chapter, I have had the feeling that I am too feminist for Bessie Head. It has been a strange experience and has made me think very deeply about how feminism, or at least what I think of as feminism, is central to how I am: American, white, educated, middle class . . . and female.

I must have been an miserable teenager for my mother to deal with. When I was in high school, I discovered *Ms.* magazine. I probably started reading it at the same time that Bessie Head became acquainted with it. But whereas Bessie Head was put off by all the anti-man jargon, all I could see was that my mother was living some kind of feminist's nightmare: high school graduate housewife with five children, a stay-at-home mother who later worked in a dead-end, woman's job as a cashier at a supermarket. I swore—to myself, but perhaps loud enough for her to hear, and feeling hopeless at the same time that a similar end was inevitable for me—that I would not end up "like that." But how was "that"? Devoting herself to her family?

Not that I ever doubted my mother's devotion. When I was a teenager, it was precisely her devotion that horrified me. Of course, I never seemed to notice my father's devotion, but it was there, especially when I needed to be fetched in the early hours of the morning. I had to get quite a bit older to understand that being devoted to others is not such a bad thing, and that most successful lives demonstrate that devotion to some degree. My parents were devoted to each other, and my father still is devoted to my mother, in many respects, almost twenty years after she died. I was even older before I realized that devoting her life to her children did not mean that my mother had abandoned everything else in her life.

I see now why Bessie Head was put off by feminism, but I cannot ignore the importance of the 1970s in shaping my own ideas of justice and equality. Reading Bessie Head has helped me to reconcile the feminist side of myself with the side that was shaped by my somewhat traditional mother and by my father, and I can see now that they are both important. I even think that in the end, they strive for the same thing. Perhaps I have been helped to understand this particular contradiction by being in a different culture than "my own" for so long. I serve tea and scones at funerals with women who are powerful in their fields but who do not see a contradiction for themselves when they discuss social policy while handing out refreshments.

Parenthood is a fact of many people's lives—and I mean parenthood and not motherhood, because the best characters in Bessie Head's novels include both men and women and they take care of others as well as themselves. Makhaya, Gilbert, Maria, and Paulina in *When Rain Clouds Gather*; Dikeledi in *Maru*; Elizabeth, Tom, and the Eugene man in *A Question of Power*; and Dikeledi and Paul Thebolo in "A Collector of Treasures": these are but the most obvious. The strength that is required to be a responsible parent is one way people face their failings, their burdens, and their obligations, but truly looking out for yourself means looking out for others, too, and only through that responsibility can come true redemption.

# 4

# "Each Man Is Helpless before Life"

*I had some lovely dreams. Some white people whom I really loved used to appear as black people or with my complexion. I used to think that this was a sign to me to overcome any dislike I might feel as far as they were concerned. I write freely about this because I feel you belong somewhere among that group and then, deeper still it is not really the black skin my dream indicates but the goodness of the heart of those individuals—that above all they are perfect already.*

KMM 74 BHP 7, n.d., probably end November 1969, to Paddy Kitchen

It is a cliché that beauty is only skin-deep, and of course many things about human beings are only skin-deep. Bessie Head was shocked to discover that black people could mistreat other "lesser" black people just on the basis of their appearance. This quotation, and her novels, illustrate her firm belief that appearance, whether racial or gendered, was a negligible aspect of human relationships. Her characters have mixed-up identities, and only when they ignore those aspects of themselves are they able to form meaningful friendships with the people they live and work with.

If gender was irrelevant for Head, then so too was skin color. What mattered was how a person treated other people, and appearance does not guarantee goodness. Black or white, every single person lives and every single person dies. Our lives are unique, like our deaths too, and what matters is how we live our lives, not how we look while doing so.

Head recognized very early the importance of what links people together, and in the following paragraph (written in 1965), we can see already her deep aversion to inflicting pain, to use one's own advantage (however that advantage may be gained) to exercise power and control:

> If I understand the causes of my own pain it prevents me from inflicting pain on others. If I see in myself so clearly and with a shuddering horror the malice, weakness, extreme vulnerability and ignorance, I am frozen, immobile; for each demented face in the battlefield around me is my own face. Where may one flee to escape the destruction? The cause of my pain is that I am an inextricable part of the conflict. ("Africa" 143)

These statements represent, I think, Head's first rejection of power politics, but also her own recognition that she is culpable because susceptible. We are all susceptible, and therefore we are also culpable. It is not a question of gender or race; it is a question of evil and weakness. We must fight in order to live.

John Mbiti, in *African Religions and Philosophy*, wrote that "In traditional life, the individual does not and cannot exist alone except corporately" (106). This idea of the corporate individual is central to Bessie Head. Her protagonists must reconcile within themselves this fundamental tension and recognize their place in the community, but they must do so without compromising their individual integrity. The kind of reconciliation about which Head wrote was unusual in much African writing, as Kolawole Ogungbesan wrote in 1980:

> Modern African writing tends, indeed, to equate the achievement of individuality with the process of alienation—the novels of Achebe, Ngũgĩ, Armah, for example, tend to focus on the breaking of ties with family, class and country. Contemporary African writers leave us, not with a realization of Man's crucial though problematic dependence on others, but with a sharpened awareness of individual separateness. But in Miss Head's novels the measure of the individual lies in the amount of work he accomplishes under back-breaking conditions, just as his acceptance by his fellowmen lies in his sharing with them their labor and dreams as they struggle to wrest a living from their hard-yielding earth. (211)

In a letter to Randolph Vigne (October 27, 1965), Head wrote that "I have always just been myself and there's nothing so wonderful in that" (*A Gesture of Belonging* 10). There is certainly "nothing so wonderful" in being Elizabeth in *A Question of Power*. The intensity of Elizabeth's alienation and of the invasion of her body and mind are painful, and many critics would probably agree with Gillian Eilersen when she wrote in *Thunder behind Her Ears* that *When*

*Rain Clouds Gather, Maru,* and *A Question of Power* are an "unconventional trilogy" in which "the movement is inward rather than forward" (176).

I also used to agree with this statement, in spite of the oddly contradictory nature of Elizabeth's final gesture of belonging. When my friend Kirsten was reading a draft of my dissertation, she commented on this contradiction, and I thought about it for a very long time. Again I turn to Olaussen, who instead believes that the trilogy represents a movement from questions of identity to questions of community (14). The contradiction can be summed up in Olaussen's argument, that the outsider must become a stranger in order to integrate into the community (98), and it is represented in the constant struggle between village as a unified entity and the individuals (or strangers) who comprise it.[1] Exile and migration promise a new beginning, but they must both start with a social death, "a realisation of complete placelessness" (239).

Desiree Lewis has noted the importance of social environment in the three novels and especially in *A Question of Power.* Discussing Boris Pasternak's importance for Bessie Head, she wrote of Pasternak's "embattled individual, driven by visions of justice, passion and freedoms that transcend social prescriptions" (*Living on a Horizon* 77) but also noted that "[i]n the same way that many of Head's characters do, Pasternak's migrate from a disintegrating world that offers little hope for their self-determination to make new lives in inhospitable worlds that they seem to build from scratch" (78), as do the people of Golema Mmidi (*When Rain Clouds Gather*) and Motabeng (*A Question of Power*). Arthur Ravenscroft wrote, more bluntly, that "Bessie Head makes one realize often how close is the similarity between the most fevered creations of a deranged mind and the insanities of deranged societies" (184). But in a letter to Charles Larson, Head noted that as soon as people have something in common to think about or do, they stop worrying about race and other insanities:

> In a racial sense, I found black people very much like white people here.
> People identify with their own. As soon as two white people get together
> they talk in a way that excludes an outsider. Black people in a predominantly

---

1 Olaussen wrote, "Head finally returns to the insight of the stranger within, the 'kaleidoscope of identities,' [quoting Kristeva, *Strangers to Ourselves*, 14, New York; Columbia UP, 1991] and also the shared destiny of us all as strangers" (145). We are all inevitably strangers to each other.

black community do exactly the same . . . When I moved on to the rural development side, the normal barriers were broken down because people's attention had been directed to other things like mutual community service, ideals and both black and white people started to confide in me quite naturally—that is how the relationship between Kenosi and Tom are [*sic*] developed, in a quite natural way, simply by picking up a spade and digging side by side. (KMM 96 BHP 8, August 5, 1974)

In a happy community, people respond according to what is present in their environment, not according to what they think they ought to be worried about.

In *The Divided Self*, Laing offered a psychological model to explain this kind of isolation. He identified two aspects of schizophrenia: the relationship a person has to the self and the relationship a person has to the world. When two "sane" people meet, each recognizes the other's identity (35). Similarly, in Foucault's view, to be sane means to participate in the same scientific, logical discourse that governs social interactions. We are able to relate to each other, according to Laing and Foucault, because we all share the same assumptions about how we ought to behave. Anyone who has ever traveled abroad will immediately recognize the truth of this, perhaps obvious, statement, but even now, in the "global community" of the twenty-first century, and especially in Africa, we still hear people say, "They don't do things the way we do!"

The clearest example of these two relationships in Bessie Head's writing occurs in *Maru*. Margaret experiences herself briefly as divided when, as the children taunt her for being a "Bushy," she thinks that she has killed a girl in the front row. When she is explaining herself to Dikeledi, she says,

> "They used to do it to me when I was a child but I never felt angry. Before you came in, I thought I had a stick in my hands and was breaking their necks. I kept on thinking: How am I going to explain her death? I thought I had killed a little girl in the front desk who was laughing, because I clearly saw myself grab her and break her neck with a stick. It was only when you started shouting that I realized I was still standing behind the table." (258)

In this example, social recognition of Margaret is explicitly being denied by the class's taunts. Laing suggested that such a split develops as a response to a world that a person perceives as hostile or even threatening, as Margaret perceives the taunts of the class.

But for Bessie Head, as I argued in the last chapter, this situation does not account for individual responsibility. In the above example from *Maru*, the incident occasions great anger in Margaret, but the subsequent split in her "self" is not just imagined; it is real. Dikeledi notices what happens to the little girl whom Margaret thinks she has killed: " 'I saw the little girl too. She put her hand to her throat when I shouted at them. I kept on looking at her because her mouth went dead white. I thought: Poor little swine. They have been taught to be brave about the wrong things and laugh about the wrong things' " (259). Bessie Head took the power of the psychic life of the human being very seriously, and that seriousness is evident in *A Question of Power*; it is real, and it manifests itself in a world that others can perceive.

That psychic life, I think, also involves the psychic life of the reader. Tom Carvlin wrote to her that "[t]he mark of the narrow man is that he can't stand to be surrounded by contradictions" (KMM 38 BHP 18, January 23, 1970), and to engage with Bessie Head is to engage with contradiction. Linda-Susan Beard referred to "disconcerting paradox" ("Bessie Head's Syncretic Fictions" 578), and Mandow described it as working the edge: you never know what side you are on in *A Question of Power*. This perspective is contrary to that of conventional literary criticism, in which a certain critical distance is assumed to be needed and maintained in order to dissect and understand the solitary object that is the text, or the author, or even the process of reading the text. But Bessie Head's writing forces a kind of intimacy on the reader—the intimacy of the stranger, as Olaussen might suggest. As I read Bessie Head and, like Tom, as I hear the voices in the novel speak to me, I start to wonder what other people think of me and my behavior. And then I start to think about how I perceive other people and what influence my own prejudices have on how I act towards them. Because everything in Bessie Head is so mixed up—in racial, gendered, and other social and psychological ways—the reader must stop and think about what is "supposed" to happen, what the expectations are and how they are destabilized and challenged. Race, gender, and, to varying degrees, other aspects of appearance influence how other people respond to us, but we ourselves control how we react to others.

In "WHAT DOES THE BOTSWANA NOVEL SAY" Bessie Head quoted a lengthy passage from Ruth Benedict's *Patterns of Culture*, in which Benedict explains how people define themselves as people and exclude others—as foreigners—from their own human world; according to Benedict this process of definition is one of the most common traits of human groups.[2] After quoting Benedict, Head closed her essay by writing, "In view of the colonial experience, in view of all that we have learned of the apartheid system in South Africa (which appears no different from Ruth Benedict's outline of the behaviour of primitive tribes), the African writer ought to look out beyond the small closed group of tribe and nation. The writer ought to look out over the world and see mankind" (KMM 457 BHP 28). What Bessie Head is calling for is an end to looking at ourselves as part of any group, except the human one. Her call, especially for someone who grew up under apartheid and experienced its oppression and exclusion first-hand, is rare. She wrote to Alice Walker that "goodness, thank God, has nothing to do with colour" (KMM 76 BHP 6, December 22, 1974), and it reminds me of Anne Frank's statement "that people are really good at heart" (287), despite overwhelming evidence in her situation to the contrary. Given the proliferation of ideologies, it would seem that almost no one accepts Bessie Head's call.[3]

Percy Mosieleng, in an essay entitled "The Condition of Exile and the Negation of Commitment," discusses the extent to which Bessie Head's experiences in South Africa shaped her life in exile in Serowe, Botswana.

---

2 The passage from Benedict's *Patterns of Culture* is quoted below. (Benedict was writing in 1934.)

Now modern man has made this thesis [our own local ways] one of the living issues in his thought and in his practical behaviour, but the sources of it go far back in to what appears to be, from its universal distribution among primitive peoples, one of the earliest of human distinctions, the difference in kind between "my own" closed group and the outsider. All primitive tribes agree in recognizing this category of the outsiders, those who are not only outside the provisions of the moral code which holds within the limits of one's own people, but who are summarily denied a place anywhere in the human scheme. A great number of tribal names in common use, Zuñi, Déné, Kiowa, and the rest, are names by which primitive peoples know themselves, and are only their native terms for "the human beings," that is, themselves. Outside of the closed group there are no human beings. And this is in spite of the fact that from an objective point of view each tribe is surrounded by peoples sharing in its arts and material inventions, in elaborate practices that have grown up by a mutual give-and-take of behaviour from one people to another.

Primitive man never looked out over the world and saw "mankind" . . . From the beginning he was a provincial who raised the barriers high. Whether it was a question of choosing a wife or of taking a head, the first and important distinction was between his own human group and those beyond the pale. His own group, and all its ways of behaving, was unique. (7)

3 Remember Lewis Nkosi's comment that her characters did not engage sufficiently with the liberation struggle.

What Mosieleng does, in the course of his discussion, is assert that, in essence, Bessie Head was not black enough. He wrote, "The visionary element that has informed her work, it is submitted, is a consequence and realization of her wilful denial of the existence of a social and ethnic environment, which is the village of Serowe and its people" (52). He faults Head for not learning Setswana, not associating with Batswana, and adhering solely to Western aesthetics, for example, not reading African writers (56–58). These specific criticisms can be countered as factually inaccurate: she attempted to learn Setswana, but found it very difficult (and she probably understood more than she admitted to); she associated with Batswana, as is clear from her letters; and she was financially constrained to read whatever people sent her or what she could get at the libraries (African literature was and continues to be difficult for many in rural areas to obtain). However, there is a more fundamental issue: Mosieleng's argument ignores Bessie Head's own desire to look beyond tribe and nation, a desire she expressed on numerous occasions and not just in the essay on Botswana novels. She objected strongly to being labeled an African writer and being consigned to the ghetto that would only allow her to write about "African issues." Rather, she saw Serowe (and she did see it and write of its existence[4]) as a microcosm of the world at large, with some problems peculiar to it—that were largely, in her view, caused by tribalism—and with some problems that were more universal. She rejected any accusation that she was not black enough, or white enough, or anything enough.[5]

In another essay, "Why Do I Write?," Head states that she does so because she has "authority from life to do so" (57). Here, in effect, is her answer to Mosieleng and to others who would tell her what to do:

---

4 All of her novels, beginning with *When Rain Clouds Gather*, show a very clear awareness of issues of Botswana life: land occupation, local politics, gender relations, etc.

5 In the postscript to a letter to Patrick Cullinan (October 3, 1965), she wrote, "Someone said to me: 'Oh, you are writing about Africa? You haven't the traditional background. You're a Coloured. You only talk English—therefore you identify yourself with the whites. You must be writing nauseating little books about Africans'" (*Imaginative Tresspasser* 80). Later, in the same letter, she wrote, "I sort of knew a lady; so intelligent who was so happy to be blacker than me. It wore me to pieces" (81).

I admit that my reading background and influences are international but I would worry if limitation could be placed on the African personality and that only certain kinds of writers could properly represent the African personality. All my characters are black but I reserve for them the charm of being unpredictable and highly original. I would dread to be faced with a dark dungeon called the "proper" and recognisable African and that this should be the standard character one would find in an African novel. There is the urge towards a kind of closed-door nationalism in independent Africa, an urge to reject the colonial experience. But this is not possible. The African personality has been enlarged and changed by the colonial experience. I am not bad on Western civilisation. I simply have a door that stands open and characters that startle and enchant my readers. (58–59)

In other words, Bessie Head's authority to write came from more than African life, even if it started there. She actively rejected African nationalism and the type of corrupt new wealth that it seemed to be spawning:

I dislike rich African men. You can hear the food they guzzle, the enormous amount of sex they guzzle, in their voices. They make no pretence to anything else . . . At first I made a big blunder. I was very eager to have an African identity, as a writer but I did not have African values, the tendency to praise the wrong things for material gain, and the wrong people because they were the open sesame to glory; the tendency to hurt life and not know they are hurting life because they just grin all the time and behind that grin hide mental cunning and evil. Those things were a nightmare to me in this country until I learned that it doesn't matter where a human being lives, as long as his contribution to life is constructive, not destructive. (KMM 25 BHP 4, February 28, 1973, to Beata Lippman)

Later, in a letter to Nikki Giovanni, she wrote that

my experiences in A QUESTION OF POWER are not some universal God or the Devil, but a form of evil black people live with as a matter of course. They have been through all I wrote down, are terrified of it but it is part of the African way of life. Those demons in my book are simply Africans and not universal persons as I said and their powers are easily acquired as part of the scheme of things here. (KMM 75 BHP 17, April 4, 1974)

Of course, Bessie Head learned her lessons in a racially oppressive system. In a brief correspondence with Langston Hughes, she described her own racial attitudes at the time. In her first letter to Hughes, dated October 10, 1960, she wrote that "[w]hat must be said must be said directly. That the solution to South Africa—lies in the hands of the Non-whites" (9); later, on January 9, 1961, she asked Hughes what he thought about John F. Kennedy, and wrote, "I don't know whether I like him or not because I don't like and trust any White people" (14).[6] But by the time she wrote *When Rain Clouds Gather,* she was beginning to rethink her ideas and to see problems not in terms of race only, because oppression comes in more forms than white colonial ones. While it is true that Makhaya and Elizabeth are made to suffer in a racially oppressive system, it is equally true that they then find themselves in societies where oppression does not have easy racial boundaries, although the nature of the oppression seems unchanged. The oppressors in the trilogy are black. The problem must, therefore, be something else.

Head's protagonists experience themselves much the way Laing described: they are alienated because South African life creates an untenable condition of "permanent nervous tension" (*A Question of Power* 19) for "Coloureds"[7] and blacks. In 1990, Roger Berger described the situation as follows: "It is the colonial encounter with the whites . . . that serves as the origin . . . of her psychopathology. This trauma locates its origin not in the Freudian family romance but first in the general condition of apartheid and then in the specific confrontation with the white" (35). In general, this understanding of the origins of the confrontation with power in Bessie Head

---

6  By the middle of May the same year, however, she was living in Sea Point, Cape Town, with a white German woman, Cordelia Guenther, with whom she apparently had a very strong, if brief, intellectual and emotional connection.

7  The term "Coloured" was used by the South African apartheid system to denote people whose ancestors were European and African. However, there is also a well-established Cape Coloured community, and Coloured communities in other parts of South Africa, who have been "Coloured" for a long time, in other words, people of mixed-race backgrounds whose ancestors became "mixed" hundreds of years ago and who form a distinctive cultural and linguistic group. In Botswana, it can mean anyone whose parents are from different racial backgrounds, although there were for a long time established Coloured communities here, too. Bessie Head, although officially classified as "Coloured," would not have belonged to any Coloured community in South Africa because her parents were not themselves Coloured (as far as can be determined), and she would not have belonged to any Coloured community in Botswana (or any community, for that matter) because she was a foreigner.

is true, but it is also limited. In all three of the novels, the tormenters are black, not white, although the shadow of apartheid certainly permeates *When Rain Clouds Gather* and *A Question of Power*. In a letter of February 2, 1979, to Jane Grant (KMM 71 BHP 30), Bessie Head describes the treatment she received from other people in Serowe and insists that the horror of *A Question of Power* comes from Botswana, not South Africa (see also September 7, 1978, letter to Jane Clegg, KMM 73 BHP 9). Berger's statement overlooks a fundamental aspect of what Bessie Head wants us to really get: that ultimately race, any race, is only an excuse.[8] The problem of power is much more deeply embedded in social patterns and even in individuals, and race is not really a useful category in trying to figure out the nature of the relationship between an individual and his or her society. As I considered in the last chapter, through Elizabeth's relationship as mother to her son, responsibility is much more useful, if just as vulnerable to exploitation. In this chapter, I will consider the notion that the representation of people's racial identity and what they expect is completely— and I think deliberately—mixed up.

In her three best-known novels, Head examines the relationship of the individual to the community in ways that are, or at least were at the time I wrote my dissertation, possibly unique in African literature. Head's outcast characters find themselves in situations where they must challenge the definitions that divide them from others and confront the social processes that have defined their difference. As her characters reforge and reconfigure their identities, Head explores the ambiguous nature of human being and community until in *A Question of Power*, Elizabeth's epiphany recognizes the necessity of both.

---

8 Dobrota Pucherova has recently looked at Bessie Head's juvenilia in order to understand how Head's identity as an anti-apartheid writer was shaped by her racial identity ("A Romance That Failed: Bessie Head and Black Nationalism in 1960s South Africa"). Pucherova argues that Head was equally alienated by the young discourse of Black Nationalism. She identifies the extent of Head's "otherness" as incorporating not only oppression by the whites, but also by blacks, for whom she was not really African (having no African culture to ground herself in), and by "Coloureds," for whom she was not really brown enough (having no links to the Cape Coloured community as a first-generation mixed-race person). Pucherova mainly argues that Head claims a "universal human identity" as a survival strategy (119) and that both gender and racial discourses are important tools in her dismantling of both apartheid and black nationalist ideologies. I am most interested in her analysis of the juvenilia in this context, since, despite Head's statement that she didn't trust white people, it supports my conteniton that race had to become irrelevant in her own vision.

In *When Rain Clouds Gather*, Makhaya crosses into Botswana illegally and settles in Golema Mmidi. When he crosses the border from South Africa into Botswana, he expects to leave behind the tribalism[9] that prevented people from existing as human beings in South Africa. South African tribalism has multiple facets, of course: the tribalism of the apartheid regime itself, which divides people into categories and assigns privileges and penalties according to the categories, and the tribalism of the townships, which dictates that Zulus stick up for each other and Sothos stick up for each other (and so on), a state of tension and conflict that the apartheid bureaucracy fosters by dispensing or withholding privileges. Makhaya has been socialized by the standards of South African society, standards he wants to escape. When he flees, he rejects the South African social standards, but he carries with him the emotional legacy of the permanent nervous tension: "His nerves weren't so good, too easily jangled by the irritations of living. In fact, the inner part of him was a jumble of chaotic discord, very much belied by his outer air of calm, lonely self-containment" (1). The permanent nervous tension is of course also racial in origin; Makhaya is a black man who has been fighting against the oppression of a white state whose policies are founded on a belief in the inferiority of black people.

The community to which Makhaya escapes is in the process of defining itself and forging itself in the face of the kind of tribalism that he fled, and this community embraces people from different tribes and different races. The villagers have been galvanized by the enthusiastic presence of a white development worker, but they have also been steadily demoralized by the manipulations of their own (black) chief, a man who uses tribe and class as exclusionary concepts to keep the villagers under control and under his heel. This is a different kind of tribalism from the racially based apartheid society Makhaya knows; it is based less on race and more on status: the chief and his cronies try to divide the society according to insiders and outsiders in more or

9 The word "tribalism" is used in Africa in a number of different ways. Mbiti used it to refer to the unity and allegiance of clan and family groups. It can refer to a divisive attitude in conflict with nationalism. Tribalism in Botswana refers to the mostly friendly but sometimes hostile rivalries that exist between the different tribes (*merafe*) and other ethnic groups of Botswana. The rivalries are friendly when there is enough to go around, but they can turn hostile when a scarcity of resources fosters stiff competition.

less the same way that Ruth Benedict described in the passage that Bessie Head quoted in "WHAT DOES THE BOTSWANA NOVEL SAY."

The villain in *When Rain Clouds Gather* is the local chief Matenge, who, along with some other independence politicians, is most interested in exploiting the villagers for his own personal gain. Bessie Head wrote in "Social and Political Pressures that Shape Writing in Southern Africa" that one thing that surprised her when she arrived in Botswana was discovering that black people could exploit and oppress other black people in the same way that whites oppressed blacks: "I knew the language of racial hatred but it was an evil exclusively practised by white people. I therefore listened in amazement as Botswana people talked of the Basarwa whom they oppressed: 'They don't think,' they said. 'They don't know anything' " (69).

Makhaya is the first expression of this surprise. He recognizes the power games that Matenge and his sidekick Joas Tsepe play, but he is also unexpectedly sympathetic to Matenge's loneliness: "[O]ne look at the face of Matenge instantly aroused his sympathy. It was the face of a tortured man" (69). Makhaya recognizes the symptoms of loneliness because he too suffers from loneliness, but Matenge "had only experienced the storms and winters of life, never the warm dissolving sun of love" (69). Matenge's treatment of the villagers only exacerbates his own condition, but that does not prevent Makhaya from feeling sympathy for someone who must be so deeply unhappy.

Makhaya's contradictory and confusing emotions begin to be sorted out by both Dinorego and especially Mma-Millipede, with whom he finds himself in a painful discussion about his status as the "Black Dog": " 'Life is only torture and torment to me and not something I care to understand' " (144). Makhaya wants to get rid of the hollow feeling inside him. When Mma-Millipede asks him what a Black Dog is, he replies that he is a "sensation":

> "He awakens only thrills in the rest of mankind. He is a child they scold in a shrill voice because they think he will never grow up. They don't want him to, either, because they've grown too used to his circus and his antics, and they liked the way he sat on the chair and shivered in fear while they lashed out with the whip. If Black Dog becomes human they won't have anyone to entertain them any more. Yet all the while they shrieked with laughter over

his head, he slowly became a mad dog. Instead of becoming human, he has only become a mad dog, and this makes them laugh louder than ever." (145)

Anticipating in an eerie way Elizabeth's experiences in *A Question of Power*, Makhaya here describes the psychological and emotional consequences of the tribalism of South Africa. What he seeks is a way to fill the hollow place inside himself, a way to be not a Black Dog or a mad dog, but a man.

Mma-Millipede responds that he needs faith, the ability to see good in spite of "the great burden of life": " 'You must never, never put anyone away from you as not being your brother. Because of this great burden, no one can be put away from you'" (146).[10] As she tries to understand the anger that drives Makhaya, she explains that the white man does not have control over the "deeper mystery" of life: " 'Whether good or bad, each man is helpless before life. This struck my heart with pity. Since I see all this with my own eyes, I could not add to the burden by causing sorrow to others. I could only help. That is why I cannot put anyone away from me as not being my brother'" (148). Dinorego earlier expresses a similar sentiment: " 'In this world are born both evil and good men. Both have to do justice to their cause. In this country there is a great tolerance of evil. It is because of death that we tolerate evil. All meet death in the end, and because of death we make allowance for evil though we do not like it'" (24). Both Mma-Millipede and Dinorego help Makhaya to understand that this contradiction is both inevitable and to be pitied. Makhaya's strength is that he deals with all people the same way, as both Mma-Millipede and Dinorego believe we should.

Makhaya surprises himself by making friends quickly and easily with a white British development worker, Gilbert Balfour. When Gilbert confesses his affection for Dinorego's daughter Maria, Makhaya finds himself warming towards Gilbert: "There might have been so many things that could have stood up as a barrier between a possible friendship, like Makhaya's background and his distrust and dislike of white people. Instead, he found himself confronted by a big man who allowed himself to be bullied by a small woman" (31–32). Gilbert, too, " 'could do with a friend around here'" (32). Makhaya is also surprised by his reactions to the local colonial official, George Appleby-Smith.

10　Mma-Millipede's statement recalls the pain that Head wrote about in "Africa" in 1964 (143).

After Appleby-Smith asserts that he'll " 'still stick my neck out for you' " (65) in response to Makhaya's angry insistence that he would always do what is right whether it suits Appleby-Smith or not, Makhaya "remained where he was some minutes longer. If there was anything he liked on earth, it was human generosity" (65). He finds that generosity in two white men.

In this environment, Makhaya is forced to articulate his own desire for a world in which tribe, race, and so on really do not matter, but in doing so he must also confront his own prejudices. Golema Mmidi is a collection of people who, like Makhaya, do not fit in anywhere. The affiliations that are created in Golema Mmidi spring from another source: a common interest in agriculture and cattle farming, a common distaste for the tribal politics of Chief Matenge and Joas Tsepe, and a common experience of having "ended up" in Golema Mmidi, which "was not a village in the usual meaning of being composed of large tribal or family groupings. Golema Mmidi consisted of individuals who had fled there to escape the tragedies of life" (18). The people of Golema Mmidi are in the process of defining their social identity in the face of an entrenched power represented by Joas Tsepe and Chief Matenge (who act against refugees and the old colonial order), a power that would like to maintain its grip.

Makhaya ends up there, too, and gets tied down before he can move on. Against the background of a village fighting the stinginess of its chief, Makhaya finds generosity. A village of outcasts makes him feel that he belongs because he shares their work and they welcome his help. Gilbert asks him to teach the women to grow tobacco because Makhaya's Setswana is better, and he accepts. The women are uneasy at first, "but once it struck them that he paid no attention to them as women, they also forgot he was a man and became absorbed in following his explanations" (119). Makhaya's developing relationship with the women he teaches demonstrates also the possibilities for reconfiguring personal, not only social, identity. Makhaya treats the women the only way he knows how, as intelligent beings, something they are not accustomed to, and his honesty enables them to be themselves. He befriends Gilbert for the same reasons. In these examples, gender and race are both made irrelevant because of the way that people treat each other. Leloba Molema describes it this way: "Makhaya refuses to inhabit the 'alien point of view' that he is 'Other.' He reciprocates by positing himself as 'the One,' thus confronting face to face the white Matenges and the black Matenges with the necessary correlative unit" (33)—that is, himself as he understands himself—rather than allowing their perceptions of him to get in the way of his sympathy or his antipathy.

In *Maru*, Margaret's tribal affiliations are equally tenuous. She is a "Masarwa,"[11] a member of the outcast of Botswana; she is adopted into the white tribe upon the death of her mother, and is commonly mistaken for a member of another tribe, the "Coloured" one. Margaret's socialization is in fact more like antisocialization because she has no sense of social belonging: her classmates' torment (232) reinforces her affiliation to a group within which she does not live and which is completely alienated from Tswana society. She has no tenable position in society.

But Margaret generally retains her sense of emotional and physical continuity and expresses herself honestly. After the trip to Dilepe, when the driver drops her at the station where she is to be collected, he takes her under his wing: he "made a great fuss about ordering her food, insisting that the knife and fork be carefully wiped. It was the stricken, helpless look on her face that so touched his heart" (236). Margaret's personal integrity and her willingness to open herself to others enable her not only to manage her pain (which gets expressed periodically in one abrupt tear) but also to connect spiritually with two important figures in Dilepe, Dikeledi and Moleka. These two people, in turn, foster her happiness in Dilepe: she is known as "the friend of Mistress Dikeledi" (301) and Moleka brings "half suns glowing on the horizons of her heart" (301). Her tormenters trained Margaret to be "irredeemably alone"; so did her teacher. Therefore, Margaret takes what she is offered and accepts as they are the relationships that are offered to her; after all, her teacher Margaret Cadmore Senior taught her to accept the things—gifts—that she casually

---

11 Head deliberately uses this term to describe Margaret, although she knew it was derogatory; in other situations, she used Mo/Basarwa:

> Maru was put together in a haphazard way. [The] Batswana . . . despise [the Basarwa] as an inferior form of human life. 35,000 members of the tribe live almost beyond reach in the Kalahari desert. A portion of the book was given to me by a British agricultural officer who worked on the edge of the desert. He found two Basarwa children working as slaves at a Batswana cattlepost. He took the two children into his home and sent them to school. He also wrote me letters for two years about his day to day life with the children, the attitudes of the people to them, the mockery and laughter that generally accompanied the sight of a Mosarwa person. (KMM 71 BHP 24, July 26, 1978, to Jane Grant)

threw away: " 'I used to feel myself catching them, and that is how I learned' " (295). Margaret's behavior is utterly genuine.

Elizabeth's background is similar to Margaret's, although her situation and behavior are more like Makhaya's. Because of the circumstances of her birth, she is assigned to a racial category to which she has no kinship affiliations whatsoever: any family she might claim belongs to a tribe from which she is institutionally barred (black father, white mother). Her ties to the "Coloureds" are as tenuous as Margaret's are to the San and the whites because she does not have ancestral or familial ties to the Coloured community. In both *Maru* and *A Question of Power*, the familiar racial categories are so mixed up that their meaninglessness and absurdity become obvious. Neither Elizabeth nor Margaret behaves as they could be expected to behave because they have not grown up inside of their "proper" communities, which for Elizabeth in any case does not really exist. The prejudices that Makhaya must unlearn are exposed in the two subsequent novels to be, in essence, chimaeras—fantasies. In a different way, too, both Margaret and Elizabeth are chimaeras: creatures made up of different parts.

In Elizabeth's South Africa, "you did not know why white people there had to go out of their way to hate you or loathe you. They were just born that way, hating people, and a black man or woman was just born to be hated" (19). In that South Africa, racial oppression and alienation was legal and institutionalized, and Elizabeth had "lived the back-breaking life of all black people in South Africa. It was like living with permanent nervous tension" (19). These circumstances characterize the origins of her suffering, but such laws as the Immorality Act of 1927, which made sexual relations outside of marriage between people of different races illegal, and the Prohibition of Mixed Marriages Act of 1949, which made such marriages illegal, mean that the "permanent nervous tension" is also part of Elizabeth's very birth and physiology: she is a South African who does not belong anywhere in South Africa because her white mother was incarcerated in an insane asylum and because her father was the black stable hand.[12] She is the visual manifestation

---

12  It is necessary at this point to remember that Bessie Head the author is not the same person as her creation Elizabeth. The details of Head's origins are not clear, but these are the facts for Elizabeth.

of a relationship characterized by transgressive female sexual behavior across the color bar.

As the physical representation of a white social nightmare, Elizabeth is denied nearly all claims to membership in her society and even in her family: "'First they received you from the mental hospital and sent you to a nursing-home. A day later you were returned because you did not look white. They sent you to a Boer family. A week later you were returned'" (17). Even at school, she is ostracized: "The other children soon noticed something unusual about Elizabeth's isolation periods. They could fight and scratch and bite each other, but if she did likewise she was locked up" (16). Elizabeth is the visible, tangible, living manifestation of something that white racism in South Africa (or any racism anywhere) finds unbelievable, unacceptable, and unbearable: first, that a black person should have any humanity at all, and second, that a white woman could see that humanity in a black man.

In *Maru*, Margaret's existence presents a similar problem for the black community, and her life contains much the same kind of tension that Elizabeth experiences. Head herself said *Maru* "*definitely* tackles the question of racialism because the language used to exploit Basarwa people, the methods used to exploit them, the juxtaposition between white and black in South Africa and black and Basarwa in Botswana is so exact" (Interview 11). Her surprise at the existence of this kind of racism, and her eventual identification of the same problem in all kinds of oppression, finds its first expression in the nature of Matenge's personality in *When Rain Clouds Gather*, possibly its most sinister expression in the character of the "real" African man Dan in *A Question of Power*, but perhaps its most obvious expression in *Maru*.

Margaret is an educated "Masarwa," a "Bushman," a person many Batswana believe is capable only of servitude:

There was no one in later life who did not hesitate to tell her that she was a Bushman, mixed breed, half breed, low breed or bastard. (230)

What did it really mean when another child walked up to her and, looking so angry, said: "You are just a Bushman"? In their minds it meant so much . . . She had no weapons of words or personality, only a permanent silence and a face which revealed no emotion, except that now and then an abrupt tear would splash down out of one eye. (232)

That the brilliance was based entirely on social isolation and lack of communication with others, except through books, was too painful for the younger Margaret ever to mention. (233)

As Pete, the principal of the school where she teaches, says of her, " 'How the hell did she get *in*? . . . She couldn't possibly have got there on her own brains' " (253).[13] An "educated Masarwa" simply cannot be; Margaret, like Elizabeth, is a physical and intellectual representation of a social impossibility, and the fact and the impossibility, simultaneously, of her existence, also like Elizabeth's, expose the real absurdity of the social morality. Bessie Head is mixing everything up.

Elizabeth is alienated from her own experiences in the way she perceives and expresses the things that happen to her. Whereas Makhaya understands very well the mechanisms of apartheid-style oppression and is able to recognize it in people like Chief Matenge, rather than the colonial officer George Appleby-Smith, Elizabeth denies any desire to identify as anyone. Elizabeth does not aspire to the false goal of whiteness nor to the equally false goal of blackness. She presses no claims on any group because, like Margaret, she has never felt entitled to claim anything. The result is that she wants to live somewhere, alone, believing that she likes to be alone and that she does not like people.

More important, however, are the two facts of Elizabeth's situation: like Makhaya, she is tormented by African figures, but unlike Makhaya, she has internalized white attitudes towards Africans, attitudes which she expresses most explicitly at the shop and in the hospital:

The insistent hiss, hiss of horror swamped her mind: "You see," it said. "You don't really like Africans. You see his face? It's vacant and stupid. He's slow-moving. It takes him ages to figure out the brand name of the radio. You never really liked Africans." (51)

"I'm not an African. Don't you see? I never want to be an African. You bloody well, damn well leave me alone!" (181)

---

13  This sentence expresses a belief that is unfortunately still extremely common: I know personally of numerous occasions where someone expressed astonishment that a San would be capable, for example, of doing university work.

But when the doctor at the hospital speaks to her conspiratorially about Botswana, "The shock of being thought of as a comrade racialist . . . abruptly restored a portion of her sanity" (184).[14] Elizabeth's perception of herself is at odds with the impression others have of her: when the doctor speaks to her as a "comrade racialist," she recognizes, at least for the moment, that her expression is also at odds with her experience.

Head further mixes up the racial map by making Dan simultaneously represent the white stereotype of the sexually depraved African man (remember the "huge, towering black penis"?) and also behave as a black oppressor who uses stereotypes of Africans to belittle someone whom he does not consider "properly African" (in a rather biting critique of African nationalism). To further confuse matters, when Dan first meets Elizabeth, he gives her his card announcing that he has held the "Directorship since 1910" (115), the year the Union of South Africa was founded, thus affiliating a black man with the racist white regimes of South Africa.

Dan and Medusa criticize Elizabeth for being not black enough, in the manner that Dobrota Pucherova suggests that Head herself encountered in the discourse of young African nationalism.[15] Elizabeth's experience of alienation has been so complete that she refuses to use her position as newcomer to establish ties in the projects at Motabeng—unlike Makhaya, who is able to accept the friendship of both Dinorego and Gilbert quite quickly. Elizabeth's life in a community within which she could have a tenable position is unfortunately characterized by her difficulty in making friends with other villagers: she cannot speak Setswana and so cannot even participate properly in the greeting ritual, leaving people to look at her "with a cheated air" (20). Eventually, when Eugene points out that she does not get along with the villagers, she asserts that " 'I like the general atmosphere because I don't care

---

14 I have also experienced this sort of assumed affinity when other white people assume that I hold the same ideas about blacks that they do. It is extremely disconcerting and makes me wonder if they are simply making an unwarranted assumption or if I have done something that makes them think I would agree with them.

15 "Bessie told Randolph Vigne how she had once been sent to interview Miriam Makeba when she worked as a reporter in Johannesburg. They were supposed to have lunch together, but Miriam regarded her with still, black eyes and refused to speak to her. Bessie had to go away again. Puzzled and annoyed, she asked a friend, 'What gives with that woman?' and he replied, 'She doesn't like Coloureds' " (Eilersen 149).

whether people like me or not. I am used to isolation'" (56). She *is* used to isolation; South Africa taught her that. But social isolation is not the same as being alone with yourself, and the former is not healthy while the latter is. She needs to learn love—of herself as well as of others, regardless of their race and especially regardless of hers.

In Lessing's *The Grass Is Singing*, Mary Turner's superficial socialization separates her from others just as thoroughly as the experiences of Makhaya, Margaret, and Elizabeth separate them. Lessing's novel demonstrates the shallow nature of the white settler-farmer society's code of behavior. Mary's socialization is not successful: she cannot become a true member of the community she aspires to because she does not understand the part she is supposed to play. She can only play *at* it: "The conventionality of her ethics . . . had nothing to do with her real life" (108). She lets others tell her what to do: "this woman who had had a 'good' State education, a thoroughly comfortable life enjoying herself in a civilized way, and access to all knowledge of her time (only she read nothing but bad novels) knew so little about herself that she was thrown completely off her balance because some gossiping women had said she ought to get married" (44). She has no sense of herself as a unique being; she only sees herself as others see her—as a "failed" white woman—and ignores her "real" self until too late. Because she has no sense of herself, she acts out her roles in ways that are all wrong. She behaves correctly but with the wrong people, or at the wrong moment. She develops a relationship with Moses; she flirts with Charlie Slatter (208), and she fantasizes that Tony Marston will save her because he looked at her kindly (234). Mary's socialization fails for two reasons: her own failure to understand the social dynamics of her community and that community's refusal to admit the authenticity of all its members. For these reasons, her personal existence and her social existence are both impossible.

In contrast to Mary, Elizabeth finally achieves some success because she is able to socialize herself according to her own needs. This success is reconciliation, and of course it is only possible because of the kind of village she lives in. Her suffering teaches her her own way of establishing genuine relationships, but her relationships (especially as mother and as gardener) give structure to her external life.

However, Elizabeth's method of splitting herself is not without its problems. Whereas Margaret's inner and outer lives are both part of her existence, Elizabeth's split is like a dual life, a life of the mind and a life in the village that seem to bear no relation to one another. She has no escape in art, as Margaret does, nor does she know how to explain her inner turmoil to anyone, like Makhaya, who unburdens himself to Mma-Millipede. Elizabeth's problems are manifest in her relationship with Kenosi, with whom she works well but to whom she cannot speak at the risk of destroying the relationship: "As the year once more came to an end, this time in a tumultuous roar of mental confusion, she made every effort to avoid turning around and snapping at Kenosi too, until she was forced into total silence. All Kenosi did was stare back at her with an inscrutable, severe expression" (160). Kenosi is devoted to the garden and consequently to Elizabeth's ability to make it grow (142); she needs Elizabeth's knowledge to make her own work there a success. The work relationship that they have is solid and built on mutual respect, and because Elizabeth fears damaging that relationship, she makes every effort to avoid opening her hell to Kenosi.

What Elizabeth fails to understand is that her survival as a corporate individual means that she must learn how to live and work with others and be both part of them and still herself. Kenosi (and the work in the co-op) gives her the opportunity to learn and practice that kind of behavior, even as the silence gives her the time to recapture her sense of herself. When she works with Kenosi in the garden, she strengthens the tie between them and affirms the relationship the two have built up. Her body works alongside Kenosi's, but her mind removes itself to remain alone while Elizabeth learns about her own needs and defines her situation: "When someone knows they are failing in every way, they still keep up the routine, filling in the gaps and blanks with frantic efforts to regain a health and control that aren't there" (162). Elizabeth's suffering undoubtedly comes from the fractured nature of life in South Africa, but it also facilitates her subsequent life in Motabeng.

Elizabeth, Margaret, and Makhaya forge connections tentatively. Elizabeth shuns several people's attempts to become friendly with her. Margaret does not believe that others will be her friends because she is a "Masarwa" and therefore not entitled to anything. Makhaya hopes to keep himself aloof so that he can evaluate the situation before committing himself, although he does not shun others, except Paulina, whom he rudely rebuffs. When Paulina sends Lorato with her greetings, Makhaya "looked down at the child and sent back a cruel message. 'Go and tell you mother I don't know her,' he said" (85). Ironically, Makhaya later marries Paulina, and indeed all Head's protagonists make close friends very quickly, given their fear of spending time with other people, but despite this reticence, their friendships seem inevitable. All three live the kind of solitude that makes such honest relationships possible: the friendships between Makhaya and Gilbert, Margaret and Dikeledi, and Elizabeth and Tom are all formed almost instantly. They are also interracial friendships.

Elizabeth is first "visited" in her mind by Sello, who creates a web of relationships for her and fills an emotional need—the need to be acquainted and friendly with others. Sello shows her "his interest in and affection for people" (23). He brings people into her room—poor and ordinary people— to establish her relationship to a greater humanity, but she remains incapable of making the imaginative leap to her other life. Sello is a prophet the way Mma-Millipede and Maru are prophets, able to imagine a life in which false barriers do not exist, and he serves the same function for Elizabeth that Mma-Millipede and Maru do for Makhaya and Margaret. They all exist in the real world, and they make a bridge: between Makhaya and his resistance to inclusion in village life, and between Margaret and her exclusion from village life. But Sello is also different from both Mma-Millipede and Maru: Mma-Millipede encourages Makhaya's return to human society, and Maru simply takes Margaret away. Elizabeth must make the connection between Sello and the people in Motabeng who would like to be her friends. She must learn love, "people mutually feeding *each other*" (197, my emphasis).

Through her friendship with Sello, Elizabeth is able to protect herself from exposure to the other "real" people of Motabeng, and, like Mary Turner's personas, this relationship protects her from having to have "real" external relationships. But whereas Mary Turner's personas protect her from herself, Elizabeth's "friendships" protect her from others. Elizabeth may not want to bridge the gap between herself and others, but she faces others constantly. Sello affirms her sense of self-worth in her isolation, even as Dan tries to destroy it. Sello's friendship reminds Elizabeth of her humanity, but only her other friends in Motabeng can validate it by how they construct their relationships with her. Elizabeth will never belong until she acknowledges others' claims on her, just as, for example, Mary Turner will never be an individual until she alters her complete reliance on others.

Both Margaret and Makhaya have tribal affiliations, but Elizabeth's membership in the "Coloured" community is artificial and imposed. Apartheid assigned her an identity, and thus also assigned her a community, but for her social commitments to be genuine, she needs to be herself as well as what others need. Elizabeth claims, "'I don't like people'" (51), but she cannot be whole until she sees the error of that statement. In John Mbiti's framework, that sentiment is wrong, because if Elizabeth rejects or refuses the companionship of other people, especially in her community, she must not be wholly human herself. Humans are social: we are defined by our communities, even if we are biologically discrete (*motho ke motho ka batho*). When Elizabeth remarks to Kenosi that she will roast a chicken for Christmas, Kenosi is surprised: "'You don't spend it with anyone?'" (90). What Elizabeth does not realize at the time—or perhaps she just cannot face up to it—is that the restoration of her peace of mind and experience of wholeness lies with the same people she tries to protect from herself, and not only her son.

Making such connections is important for both Margaret and Makhaya as well, because they too must find their way in the places they settle. Margaret's future is both joyful and bleak, precisely because she has been disconnected from those (Moleka and Dikeledi) who validate her social humanness. Marriage can be a way of establishing kinship and social ties,[16] but Margaret's marriage annihilates hers. In *When Rain Clouds Gather*, Mma-Millipede warns Maria about letting Gilbert get away and tells her that "'Gilbert might have become impatient and run away to England; then not only would you have lost him, but we too'" (97). Marriage does not work for Margaret the way it does for Makhaya and Gilbert because in order for her marriage to be successful, she and Maru must leave Dilepe. Margaret's sacrifice foreshadows *A Question of Power*, with its more overtly Christian imagery of suffering and resurrection.

---

16  Mine certainly has been!

The sixth chapter of *When Rain Clouds Gather* opens with the statement, "One might go so far as to say that it is strong, dominating personalities who play a decisive role when things are changing" (81). Gilbert Balfour and Paulina Sebeso are the first such dominating personalities. Dinorego describes Gilbert in near visionary terms and clearly worships his knowledge about farming and "progress": " 'I have no words to describe Gilbert, son . . . If Gilbert goes, who will pour out knowledge like rain?' " (24). His physical presence is inspiring, too:

> He was not big, he was a giant, and his massive frame made him topple forward slightly and sway as he walked . . . Life never seemed to offer enough work for his abundant energy, and his gaze forever restlessly swept the horizon seeking some new challenge, while at the same time his mind and hands could busy themselves with the most immediate and insignificant details in a continuous flow of activity like a wave. (26–27)

Gilbert is practically a force of nature, but his failings, most notably his inability to communicate well in Setswana with his fellow villagers, limit his ability to bring his grand dreams to reality. The text makes clear Gilbert's faults, but supplies him with someone whose strengths complement his: Makhaya. Together, they have the strength to forge significant improvements in the life of Golema Mmidi. Paulina, too, dominates the villagers; she is secretly admired by the women, who "followed the leadership of Paulina because she was so daring and different" (102).[17] But part of the importance of Paulina and Gilbert as dominating personalities is that they have the ability to mobilize others. The result at the end of *When Rain Clouds Gather*, when Matenge's summons to Paulina galvanizes the villagers' will, which then causes Matenge to kill himself (198–209), foreshadows the statement at the end of *A Question of Power*, and the villagers' will is, I think, an early articulation of Head's idea about the totality of all souls.

Virginia Ola noted the importance of complementarity in 1990 in her essay "Power and the Question of Good and Evil in Bessie Head's Novels." She wrote that "this complementarity functions either as the necessity for an individual

---

17  When she imperiously invites Makhaya to eat with the women, he stands up and is "relieved to see that he was a whole foot taller than" she is (123).

to realize his full potential by recognizing his own strengths and weaknesses, and thereby seeking to identify with another character who possesses what he himself lacks; it also features as two characters functioning as the positive and negative qualities of one person" (63). The first type of complementarity is plainly illustrated in *When Rain Clouds Gather* by the friendship of Gilbert and Makhaya. Ola describes Gilbert as "the rational scientist" and Makhaya as possessing the "sensitivity, trustworthiness, patience and a fascinating ability to make people do his bidding without exerting too much energy" (63). The second type of complementarity is represented in the more ambiguous characters in *Maru* and *A Question of Power*.

It is unclear how Bessie Head herself started out thinking about the nature of responsibility. It is clear that her opinions about the relationships between whites and blacks changed over time, as is reflected in the earlier quotation about John F. Kennedy, stating that she fundamentally did not trust white people and that the solution to the problems of apartheid had to be in the hands of the nonwhites. Her experiences in Botswana and the discovery that abuse of power and oppression of others was not a white prerogative brought the evolution of her thinking to the point that someone like Mosieleng could accuse her of being too immersed in the white world. But Bessie Head saw all relationships as equally important, regardless of skin color, and she was able to see the world this way because she put "the accent heavily on self-responsibility" (KMM 38 BHP 25, May 1, 1970, to Tom Carvlin). We should respect others and take responsibility for our own behavior towards them because they are human beings; if we do this, we will be obliged to give up all pretense that we have power over them. In reading Bessie Head, we have to examine how we feel about black characters who are evil and white characters who are good, and that means that we have to think about our own prejudice.

Recently I read James McBride's *The Color of Water: A Black Man's Tribute to His White Mother*. McBride, an American, writes about his white Jewish mother and about how he finally came to realize that he needed to understand his mother and her past. Near the end of the book is an extended passage in which the writer discusses his attempts (and refusals) to "find himself." One passage in particular struck me as something Bessie Head might have understood:

Being mixed is like that tingling feeling you have in your nose just before you sneeze—you're waiting for it to happen but it never does. Given my black face and upbringing it was easy for me to flee into the anonymity of blackness, yet I felt frustrated to live in a world that considers the color of your face an immediate political statement whether you like it or not. It took years before I began to accept the fact that the nebulous "white man's world" wasn't as free as it looked; that class, luck, religion all factored in as well; that many white individuals' problems surpassed my own, often by a lot; that all Jews are not like my grandfather and that part of me is Jewish too. Yet the color boundary in my mind was and still is the greatest hurdle. (205)

I realize that what Bessie Head is trying to do is Herculean.

In 1995, I wrote that Head's vision in *A Question of Power* is her most explicitly affirming. I am no longer sure I believe that. It is certainly her most powerful vision, but I now think that this vision, like much of life, is too problematic to be affirming. Elizabeth, like Makhaya, clearly rejects the kind of relationships that South African society offers in favor of the more cooperative, egalitarian relationships available to her, as epitomized by her relationships with Kenosi, a Motswana, and with Tom, a white fellow immigrant; that egalitarianism is already present too in the relationship between Makhaya and Gilbert. Even as I write this now, I struggle with these ideas and with my own faults and prejudices.

I once had occasion to think about my own prejudices when I was getting out of my car at the supermarket. An older white man was coming towards me berating the young black man who was pushing the older man's shopping cart. The man's accent was that of an Afrikaans speaker, and all of my revulsion towards white Afrikaans speakers welled up in me and I thought about intervening. Fortunately, I did not because later, when I was returning to my car and saw them again, chatting and laughing in the company of a black woman, I realized that the younger man was the older man's son, and the woman was probably his mother, and the earlier incident was more likely to be a father berating his teenaged son. Sitting in my car in the parking lot of a grocery store in Botswana in Southern Africa, with all its history of white abuse of blacks, I had to think about my own assumptions about who that white man was and what he represented, which clearly had nothing to do with who he really might be. My knee-jerk reaction made me ashamed. Not all white people are oppressors, and not all oppressed people are noble. Obviously, I still have a lot to learn. As a footnote to this story, I can add that I now see this man and his son nearly every time I go to the mall where the supermarket is located; seeing them is apparently my penance for misjudging them.

Elizabeth's suffering is not pretty—no one's is—it is violent and abusive, and learning the lessons that Sello presents for her is an epic battle that takes an incredible toll. It is also the means by which Elizabeth sheds the legacy of her South African past and comes to a new understanding of her life in Motabeng. In Elizabeth, Head embraces the dilemma that faces each person in the human community, and she bridges the gulf between Elizabeth and Motabeng, her utopia, a true "no place." Her struggle to find a place for herself in Motabeng is coincident with her struggle to understand the duality of being. Charlotte Bruner wrote of the "progression from the position of affirmation of *When Rain Clouds Gather* . . . to the uncertain, thin hope of survival through individual inner strength of . . . *A Question of Power*" (263). This statement is certainly true, but the novels also establish the coincident nature of the two problems, emotional and social: "The man's name was Sello. A woman in the village of Motabeng paralleled his inner development" (*A Question of Power* 11). Makhaya finds personal peace at the same time that he finds Paulina. Before Margaret finds happiness with Maru, she first finds it in the knowledge that Moleka loves her and that Dikeledi is her friend.

Elizabeth's friends and her son remind her that she has a place; Tom reminds her that she loves everything, even vegetables (188). His gregariousness and his sociability appeal to Elizabeth: "In every way he showed that he liked lots of company and was as carelessly gregarious as his walk. People were a blur he grasped together with wide open arms, indiscriminately" (121). That "indiscrimination" is important: it explains the importance of accepting all human relationships. Tom is the only person to whom Elizabeth tries to explain her inner world, and his generosity and wisdom mean that he can listen to her without condemning her suffering as mental illness (190). He gives Elizabeth room, and time, to talk and to express her torment to someone else. Trying to explain it to someone else means that she automatically moves away from the isolation that Dan wishes to maintain. Sello recognizes Tom's generosity and humanity, and tells Elizabeth that he loves Tom (and remember that Tom hears Sello agree with him at one point [24]). Tom, by reminding her that she loves everything, creates the conditions for her to open up to other people like Mrs. Jones (196). His generosity also sets the stage for Sello to tell her that love is not the cruelty that Dan flaunts: love is mutual, "not one living on the soul of the other like a ghoul!" (197). Elizabeth's relationship with Kenosi reflects that same principle: two people mutually helping each other, not one wielding power over the other like a tyrant. And that means everyone, including you and me.

Jean Marquard wrote that for Elizabeth, "sanity means making friends" (60). I hope to show in the next chapter that making friends is not enough, that it is only one aspect of Elizabeth's salvation. She must face the most fundamental contradiction of all: every person carries the potential for good and evil; that capacity exists even within love itself. Good and evil, like other human characteristics, do not exist independently of one another in anyone. Makhaya sees Matenge's loneliness in himself; Maru's ruthlessness serves social justice. If we can embody contradiction in our existence as corporate individuals, we can also embody contradiction in our very natures, as both good and evil. This contradiction, introduced in *When Rain Clouds Gather* and *Maru*, is confronted head-on in *A Question of Power*.

# 5

# "Love . . . Is a Touchy Thing"

*God is not our parent. He is entirely outside the stream of flesh, blood, and history which links us together. We are free! See, now, why it seems to me unlawful to found the vindication on history, and senseless to rail against God by reason of our misery.*

Cheikh Hamidou Kane, *Ambiguous Adventure* 162[1]

*How good is a good without a choice? Voodoo gods are like you and me—they fight, they love, they try to conquer death. They aren't perfect and remote like the white God and the Virgin.*

Jewel Parker Rhodes, *Voodoo Dreams: A Novel of Marie Laveau* 241

*The embarrassment of the book is that a part of it takes place on a spiritual level—people prefer to call it insanity but it is not a record of insanity as much as it is a record of the spirit.*

KMM 77 BHP 33, September 13, 1974, to Betsy Stephens

*People could not see their souls, they do not know they are divine.*

KMM 43 BHP 2, September 7, 1968, to Jean Highland

In a letter of August 26, 1974, to Randolph Vigne (*Gesture of Belonging* 187), Bessie Head noted that reviewers of *A Question of Power* ignored one of the most pivotal statements in the book: "I thought too much of myself. I am the root cause of human suffering" (191). Dorothy Driver, in a review of Head's correspondence with Vigne ("Gestures of Expatriation and Belonging"), stated that the letters help explain this "startling" statement because "a victim,

---

1 The Knight here is referring to the Islamic rather than the Christian understanding of God; the quotation seems somehow appropriate, however, because of the implied importance of self-responsibility, and despite the suggestion of distance from humankind.

being forced to become a kind of repository of all the racial hatred and other human suffering, then becomes the source of that evil" (17). Driver's statement assumes that the victim starts out "good"; the statement from *A Question of Power*, though, addresses the possibility that we do not: it reflects more closely the idea that we are born with original sin and with knowledge of good and evil. Head identifies that pivotal statement in *A Question of Power*, but other statements in the book reflect the same sentiment. Elizabeth's plea to her doctor, " 'Please help me . . . It's Sello. He's both God and the devil at the same time' " (176), does not simply express an impossible contradiction created in the fever of her own mind. That contradiction exists in every human being; indeed, it defines part of the nature of love itself.[2] Love may be divine, but it is also human. In *A Question of Power*, Elizabeth's victory over her suffering is expressed in her prophecy, which itself represents the next stage of the articulation of Head's vision: both secular and divine, ordinary and exalted.

Elizabeth's madness has been described in criticism as a journey,[3] and my dissertation of twenty years ago reflects that. I wrote then that Elizabeth underwent a kind of rite of passage in which she came to terms with the alienation she experienced in South Africa and created a new life for herself, even a new self, in the garden in Motabeng. Now I think that Bessie Head's vision is much more complex, nuanced, and decidedly spiritual, including Christian.

Many critics assert that Bessie Head rejected Christianity, and certainly her account of her experiences at St. Monica's school support that assertion: "[F]or years and years after that I harboured a terrible and blind hatred for missionaries and the Christianity which they represented, and once I left the mission I never set foot in a Christian church again" ("Notes from a Quiet Backwater I" 4). Looking at this quotation again, I notice that she identifies "the Christianity which they represented," and I wonder less at the Christian imagery that infuses her work. Nevertheless, many early interpretations of *A*

---

2  Again, this contradiction is reminiscent of Jung's shadow.
3  See, e.g., Linda-Susan Beard, "Bessie Head's *A Question of Power*: The Journey Through Disintegration to Wholeness"; Charles Larson, *The Novel in the Third World*; Margaret E. Tucker, "A 'Nice-Time Girl' Strikes Back: An Essay on Bessie Head's *A Question of Power*"; Rukmini Vanamali, "Bessie Head's *A Question of Power*: The Mythic Dimension"; and Cherry Wilhelm, "Bessie Head: The Face of Africa."

*Question of Power* in particular looked at the other religious ideas represented there in order to explain the very spiritual nature of the book.

Different understandings of spirituality in Bessie Head are possible because the figures who visit Elizabeth also represent aspects of various religious systems—Hindu, Buddhist, Christian, Greek.[4] Norman Cary even offered a Bakhtinian analysis, given "Bakhtin's anti-authoritarian religious view" (38), and, in keeping with Bakhtin's "penchant for lists" (39), he proposed "a Bakhtinian categorization of her comments about religion" (39).[5] This probably seems like an odd place to start a summary of approaches to Head and spirituality, but I am doing so because Cary's conclusions have given me a useful summary of the points I have been thinking about.

Cary's eight items lead him to make four conclusions (49) about Bessie Head's writing that are probably too ideologically rigid. First, he asserts that religion is psychological rather than revelational. Second, he states that Bessie Head rejects the idea of a transcendent God. Third, not everyone is God, only those who act in support of the oppressed. Fourth, "missionary Christianity" (missionary activity) can be both positive and negative. Of these four, only the last one captures the ambiguity of Head's vision.

First, and most importantly, to say that religion is psychological and not revelational in Bessie Head is necessarily to reduce what happens to Elizabeth to an episode of mental illness, and to read *A Question of Power* without passion is to ignore the revelations that her characters must see, and that are offered to us, too. This is my contention: it is impossible to read Bessie Head with any understanding without seeing those revelations.

Second, Head does not entirely reject the idea of a transcendent God; on occasion she yearns for one: "I wish the unknown God would walk in on me

---

4  See, e.g., Paul H. Lorenz, "Colonization and the Feminine in Bessie Head's *A Question of Power*," and Rukmini Vanamali, "Bessie Head's *A Question of Power*: The Mythic Dimension."

5  Cary proposed the following eight points concerning religious and anti-religious ideas in Bessie Head. First, "Religion originates in the human mind" (39); this is both good and bad. Second, "theological concepts" should be "concretized in human discourse and behavior" (40). Third, "Bakhtin stresses the interplay among religious ideas"; so does Head (40). Fourth, "Bakhtin associates the carnivalesque with the decentering of authority in favor of popular knowledge and power" (40). Fifth, "The central emphasis in Bakhtin is the challenge brought by the dialogic imagination to traditional monologic authority" (41). Sixth, religion is also positive (41). Seventh, there is less inclination to individualism (41). Finally, the paradigm of death and resurrection is indicative of interplay between good and evil in a human being (41).

sometime, unexpectedly and say: 'Here I am. Now love me'" (letter of August 13, 1971, *A Gesture of Belonging* 148).[6]

Third, everyone *is* God; for this reason, Bessie Head's ideas about God can be hard to accept: it is nearly impossible to love the person who oppresses you, but that experience is part of the nature of God, humanity, and life. We see this when Makhaya feels sympathy for Matenge (*When Rain Clouds Gather* 69) and when Elizabeth realizes that she "treasured her encounter with Dan" (*A Question of Power* 202). When Head asserts that God is in every human being, she is also saying that God has the capacity for evil, and that is precisely the insoluble problem, one of the things that makes Elizabeth's faith so hard.[7]

Cary was correct, however, in stating that "missionary Christianity" can be both positive and negative, but that is true of many things.[8] In "My Relationship to Botswana and South Africa as a Writer," notes for a talk she gave at the Francistown Teacher Training College in July 1975, she wrote that "I concentrated directly on people because it is only people who make people suffer . . . I am also indiscriminate about who is good and who is evil—that is a matter beyond skin colour and qualities common to all mankind" (KMM 457 BHP 25). This idea is explored in a specifically missionary context in the short story "Heaven Is Not Closed," in which a Christian convert dies a "magnificent death" (7) after she has been cast out of the church by a white missionary for marrying a traditionalist, with whom she had a very happy marriage and who did not prevent her from continuing to pray to her Christian God. Nearly ten years after that story was published, in 1985, Head wrote that "I foresee a day

---

6  Craig MacKenzie would seem to agree with Cary: "the 'religion' that Elizabeth comes to embrace is one that has no God" (154). But I disagree, since I think that the concept of God that MacKenzie refers to is that of a single entity, whereas I think Head sees God in a radically different way.

7  The other, of course, is facing the evil in ourselves.

8  Head herself several times acknowledged the importance of missionaries and Christianity in addressing the status of women. In "Despite Broken Bondage, Botswana Women Are Still Unloved," she wrote that "Christianity then presented itself as a doctrine above all traditions and mores; a moral choice freely available to both men and women and it is in this sphere that all major social reforms took place" (56), including abolition of bride price, which had the added benefit of allowing "women to lodge complaints against their husbands on their own and not through a male sponsor, as was required by custom" (57), and polygamous marriages. In "Societal Values and Women: Images vs. Real Life," she wrote that "I would say that the present position of a vast majority of women in the rural areas of Botswana is not an ideal one . . . I would suggest that the ideal of love between a man and a woman is absent in the society, that women suffer from a heritage where their humanness and individuality were always subservient to social norms" (51).

when I will steal the title of God, the unseen Being in the sky, and offer it to mankind. From then onwards, people, as they pass each other in the street each day, will turn to each other and say: 'Good-morning, God.' War will end. Human suffering will end" ("Why Do I Write" 59). We will then worship each other the way we worship our Gods.

June Campbell's Buddhist reading of *A Question of Power* and Desiree Lewis's exploration of the place of Hinduism in Head's work are also very useful. Campbell believes that the reconciliation of mind and body give a Buddhist cast to the novel, and through this reconciliation, Head challenges the validity of the physical over the mental as the only reality (66). Campbell suggests that *A Question of Power* draws us into "questioning the origins and limits of the mind itself and its multifarious manifestations" (67). Campbell concludes that suffering teaches Elizabeth something, but it is not possible to categorize what that something is (77), because there is not one question of power; instead, the novel takes the reader to "the very meaning of power itself" (78).

More recently, the Christian references in her work have been identified in other contexts. Desiree Lewis observed that chapters 4 and 12 of *A Bewitched Crossroad* show Head's fascination with the representation of Christian conversion and its attraction particularly for women in releasing them from oppressive social customs (284). And Maria Olaussen pointed out that in *When Rain Clouds Gather*, "Head introduces a religious terminology [of moral choices] but she makes it clear that she is not satisfied with how proponents of Christianity have dominated this discussion" (163).

Lauren Smith, in an article entitled "Christ as Creole: Hybridity and the Revision of Colonial Imagery in the Works of Bessie Head," identifies this trend toward multiplicity as well within the writing of Bessie Head, including in the spiritual world Head describes. But Smith also wrote, "Bessie Head's work is somehow able to contain both an anti-colonial commitment and a certain indebtedness to elements of colonial culture" (68), once again working the edge (to use Mandow's phrase) and leaving her reader with no escape. Head herself was clear about the effects of "colonial culture": "There is the urge towards a kind of closed-door nationalism in independent Africa, an urge to reject the colonial experience. But this is not possible. The African personality has been enlarged and changed by the colonial experience" ("Why Do I Write" 59).⁹

In her specific analysis, Smith looks at *When Rain Clouds Gather* and *A Question of Power*. She wrote that the world of *When Rain Cloud Gather* reflects Mma-Millipede's Christianity as much as anything (63), and that the narrative structure of the novel evokes the Biblical end of the world (64). She interprets the drought as both plague and miracle that cleanses everything in preparation for Gilbert's cattle cooperative, so that a "new Kingdom" can arise (65).

Desiree Lewis notes more generally that Head's spirituality is not very tidy (8). She makes the important point that Bessie Head was also disillusioned by authoritarian strains of Hinduism and drifted towards Buddhism: "Towards the end of her life, she was to turn increasingly to figures whom she saw as independent thinkers. In particular, she was attracted to thinkers who believed not so much in tutelage and obedience, as in encouraging their followers' spiritual development through independent introspection, observation and meditation" (86). For Head, this kind of serenity can only come from a complete association of everyone and everything with divinity.

Head's interest in Hinduism included a belief in reincarnation. In "Notes from a Quiet Backwater II," she wrote that

> [t]he canvas on which I have worked was influenced by a belief in the Hindu view of rebirth and reincarnation. Such a belief influences one to the view that each individual, no matter what their present origin or background may be, is really the total embodiment of human history, with a vast accumulation of knowledge and experience stored in the subconscious mind. (77)

In *A Question of Power*, Sello tells Elizabeth that their friendship will never end, and she asks him if "that means we are supposed to meet again in other lives?" (201); it does. In a letter to Randolph Vigne (May 14, 1966), Head wrote that "quite a lot of my previous incarnations were spent in India. When I found this out some time ago I thought deeply about the matter" (31). Eilersen

---

9  Smith also notes that the protagonist of "Heaven Is Not Closed" is a Christian happily married to an African traditionalist "without losing any of her spiritual power or goodness" (72), and despite her excommunication by a local missionary.

noted that Head believed she had in a previous incarnation been the Swami Vivekananda (*Thunder behind Her Ears* 152), and identifies a letter (KMM 38 BHP 20) in which she describes a "drama" that took place between a man named Deep Ridge and his wife, a man named Long Profile, a woman named Dan, and Bessie herself. Head summarized the story by writing, "Not to mince matters, I was the David of the Bible, who slaughtered Uriah to get his wife, Bathsheba. This Bathsheba turned up in the form of the man 'Deep Ridge' and the present wife was the great old general Uriah" (letter to Tom Carvlin, undated, probably 1970).

Eilersen also suggested (273–74) that Head associated herself with Mother Kali (one of the forms of the goddess Devi). In her notes, Bessie Head copied out the following description of Mother Kali (the quotation marks are in Head's original notes; the description appears to come from Swami Nikhilānanda's introduction to *The Gospel of Sri Ramakrishna*, but there is no source attributed on the document itself):

> . . . She combines the terror of destruction with the reassurance of motherly tenderness. She is the Cosmic Power, the totality of the universe, a glorious harmony of the pairs of opposites. She deals out death as she creates and preserves. She has three eyes, the third being the symbol of Divine Wisdom; they strike dismay into the wicked, yet pour out affection for Her devotees. Mother Kali is the Creator. Nay, she is deeper. She is the Universal Mother, the All-powerful. She takes away the last trace of ego and merges it in the consciousness of the Absolute. She is the Seed of Immortality. She stands on the bosom of her husband, Shiva, the Absolute, who lies prostrate at her feet, She appears to be reeling under the spell of wine. She is the highest symbol of all the forces of nature, the synthesis of their opposites, the Ultimate Divine in the form of woman. (KMM 457 BHP 64, undated handwritten notes, opening ellipsis in original)

It is no wonder that this description appealed to Head, given the importance of duality and the merging of opposites in Head's own writing (especially in the trilogy), given the terrible yet also tender nature of Mother Kali herself, given the images of battle and destruction that resonate in *A Question of Power*, and considering the idea of one's ego merging "in the consciousness of the Absolute."

In a letter to Mona Pehle (December 7, 1975), Head explained her understanding of two strains of Hinduism:[10]

> Roughly, the Vedanta view is that the whole universe is permeated by a feeling of holiness so in essence the discipline and training extends the title of God to all things, animate and inanimate so in effect you say: "This cup is God. This man is God. This tree is God. This stone is God. All things are God." Now, you can imagine the chaos of either having the whole universe rush into you, the chaos of complete identification with the totality of life, the chaos of feeling it as a violent experience, the sense of being lifted out of a small encasement of the body and being the universe itself? It is a discipline not suited to all temperaments and the Advaita is man's small ordered neat world: "I am man. God is a thing apart from me. I worship something apart from me." The Advaita view comes nearest to formal religion. But I like the Vedanta view: God is about the only title that can be shared, so if you know me, you would also know why I sound mad. I recklessly dispense the title in all directions. (KMM 34 BHP 21)

Head was attempting to explain the attraction for her of "Vedanta" to someone who was Christian and who engaged with her in a dialogue about Christian beliefs and personal spirituality. The "independent introspection, observation and meditation" that Lewis identifies is central to Head's own writing—because by not conceding easy answers or morals to her readers, she forces them to consider their own role in divinity. We may ultimately disagree with her, but in order to disagree, we first have to understand her.

For me, this is perhaps the biggest ongoing challenge—why I keep reading Head after more than twenty-five years—I want to understand.

* * *

Felix Mnthali, at a seminar in the Department of Theology and Religious Studies at the University of Botswana in 1991, opened his paper with the following statement:

---

10  In the passage, Bessie Head uses the terms in a way that is not quite correct, but is still found in Western usage. Vedanta (ironically, an elite strain of Hinduism) consists of Advaita Vedanta (nonduality), Vishishtadvaita Vendanta (qualified nonduality), and Dvaita Vedanta (duality). She is probably using Vedanta for Advaita Vedanta and Advaita for Dvaita Vedanta.

The fear and trembling with which a mere literary scholar approaches a topic such as the one before us now is tempered by the feeling that what unites writers and the people of God everywhere is the concept of <u>wholeness</u>. We see wholeness as the unity between body and soul; the vital link between humanity's search for transcendental "weightlessness" and the matter out of which such transcendence is to be achieved . . . The more one reads literature the more one comes away with the feeling that human beings continually restructure, rebuild, rewrite and re-read God in their own image. (1)

In this discussion, Mnthali refers to Nietzsche, Kierkegaard, and Kant to begin his examination of religious symbolism and meaning in Ngũgĩ wa Thiong'o's novels. Mnthali argues that the notion of God changes in every writer, and he asserts at the end of his discussion that what he has presented is not "a new way of looking at literature but another mode, another perspective of looking at God" (14).

So it is with Bessie Head.[11] Her letters, preserved at the Khama III Memorial Museum in Serowe, contain countless references to ways of looking at God, and they cover more than fifteen years, from her arrival in Botswana in 1964, through her hospitalizations in 1969 and 1971, and after the publication of *The Collector of Treasures* in 1977. Here, in her own words, is what she had to say.

September 28, 1964, to Patrick Cullinan

Intellectuals or thinkers believe it is a great act of courage to say there is no God. Actually, in this age it's a great act of courage to say there is a God and fully understand all the implications of saying so. When intellectuals say there is no God, they are merely confirming the materialistic trend of the age in which we live. We look inside nothing. Only outside all the time . . . It's easier to accept Karl Marx's view of the brotherhood of man than that of Jesus Christ. Jesus is almost a myth, but Karl Marx was born in 1880 something. He figured out his brotherhood of man in £.s.d. which is so much easier to understand than mystical clap-trap. Somehow, £.s.d. is no answer to me. (*Imaginative Trespasser* 24)

---

11 And at this point, "God" is no longer Christian, but much more amorphous. We are moving into untidiness.

When I was in my twenties, I thought I was being courageous by declaring myself a Marxist and rejecting all tenets of Christianity. But now I am frightened of the material trend of the world.

<u>November 29, 1967, to Robert Gottlieb</u>

Somehow, Christianity, as preached by the missionaries has failed to give this concept of power to people in Africa because the missionaries themselves failed to have a true concept of their God. I have often wondered how Jesus Christ could bear to have his name propagated by milksops when he was such a weird, strange, character, full of alarms and diversions and wit and humour. I treasure him too much to go to all these milksop churches. I like him as a Jew, in his historical setting . . . The Jews are the backbone of Christianity. Why then do men despise those who give them their Gods, even such a great and lovely God like Jesus Christ? (KMM 58 BHP 1)

<u>September 7, 1968, to Jean Highland</u>

Not even God thinks too much of himself. I told him the other day that I did not give a damn for God and all such nonsense. I only care about the freedom of the human soul. He was very pleased by this statement. I have noticed that he can terrorise people into respecting him. He is also a little bit vain. The truth is, all the hosts of heaven are down here with him. The day they know themselves and him they are going to go mad, with joy. I'll be the only one who will keep my head. I really don't give a damn who is God or the devil. All are one. (KMM 43 BHP 2)

When I read this, I am reminded of Alice Walker's *The Color Purple*, in which Shug also describes God to Celie as everything, and only wanting to be loved back, doing nice things all the time so that people will notice: "I think it pisses God off if you walk by the color purple in a field somewhere and don't notice it . . . People think pleasing God is all God care about. But any fool living in the world can see it always trying to please us back" (167). When I first read that line in Walker's novel, I had no idea what to make of it.

<u>June 11, 1969, to Randolph Vigne</u>

What I said about God in the book was related very closely with Makhaya's inner struggles. I simply want God in mankind instead of up in the sky. Put him inside a man and a man is obliged to live a noble life, where other people can depend on him to be truthful in his dealings. People brought up on Christianity think God has nothing to do with them. (*A Gesture of Belonging* 90–91)

I was brought up on Christianity and God was distant, and I could not figure out why God could tell me what to do. He was in coloring books and "somewhere" in church on Sunday, but the whole "God thing" didn't make sense in the world around me. Kindness to others was something my parents taught me, and they explained it in terms of "how would you feel if . . .." I dismissed people who did not act according to these same principles. I could not love them in the way that Head insists we must, and this is why love is so hard.

<u>January 16, 1971, to Randolph Vigne</u>

The mistake is to pray to the invisible. I never have. I have prayed to living things I can see. I distrust what I cannot see.

Divinity seems to suggest an untouchable holiness. I distrust that. There is no such thing. There is hard living, great blunders and great abdications and the people who make these lives of immensity and history are the Gods. (*A Gesture of Belonging* 135)

So do I. Even as a child, I wondered what "happened" to my bedtime prayers. Did they make it "up there"? What if God was busy? How could I find out if He heard me? This is why I find faith so difficult.

<u>August 13, 1971, to Randolph Vigne</u>

If we have to live with love, in the future, we also have to live with our friends who come in to tea. (*A Gesture of Belonging* 150)

It is one thing to sit in isolation and say: God, the unseen, I worship you. It is another to say to a living man: God, the seen, I worship you. It is like loving a prickly pear and only the very sane can love like that. (*A Gesture of Belonging* 151)

My problem is that I'm too selfish to love the people, the "prickly pears," I once dismissed.

<u>March 24, 1972, to Myrna Mackenzie</u> (regarding people "praying to something they have in their minds")

Then I thought: "They are praying to a God they will never see because there is no God like ordinary people. There is no one in heaven or hell with ordinary human kindness and decency." (KMM 23 BHP 6)

December 11, 1973, to Myrna Mackenzie

Ever since Jesus started it, there is this fatal belief that one must cast out evil spirits. My own feeling is that evil is much more subtle and eternal and more shape changing than anything else, because it is a world of all kinds of illusions as powerful, if not more powerful than creative goodness. My own feeling is that one can at best find out the principles on which it operates and see whether one dislikes it—then only can one chose. It is much harder than miracle performing which I think is an illusion too. (KMM 23 BHP 49)

October 30, 1976, to Betty Fradkin (regarding the death of a young man Fantisi who Head suggests was universally loved in Serowe)

He offered you, and you meant everyone, a form of instant love that was so simple and uncomplicated that you could do nothing but accept it. He turned and smiled at you, and you meant everyone, in exactly the same way. (KMM 15 BHP 36)

My mother was like this. When we were younger, all our friends thought our mother was great. I thought she was annoying, always fiddling with my hair, wanting to know what I was doing, where I was going, how I was. "Fine," I said, monosyllabically. But nevertheless, with what must have been heroic effort, my mother loved me. She loved everyone. That is why everyone loved her.

December 30, 1978, to Tony Hall (in response to a collection of essays by Hall called "Seek First the Kingdom of Heaven" [KMM 47 BHP 39])

I cannot solve the mystery of Jesus Christ, the demand to place implicit faith in a single, dominating personality: No one comes unto the Father, except by me. Take salvation from me alone. It's here on a plate. This has fascinated mankind. Oh They've loved it so much, but not the whole world. But its been big enough to include the whole world. I shy away from the single powerful, dominating figure. All should be Christ. As you write: If you truly follow Christ you will only be content when all are Christ.

I am ashamed of nothing because I don't want to be the Being in the Sky . . . That was why I used the D. H. Lawrence quote at the beginning of my book. "Only Man can fall from God, only Man . . ." It follows then that Man is God. That was all I was saying.

I bow to Marxism and stand close to it in the sense that it is important to feed and clothe and house mankind. No religious leader could break open that hard vicious door of the privileged few who lived on and exploited the many.

But they do not acknowledge man's holiness. They will kill and kill and kill and I hate their arrogance. Perhaps I imagine a world where people see they are God and the greeting changes and people say to each other: "Good-morning God." You couldn't possibly kill God if it was you, could you? You couldn't possibly exploit or do any evil to God and God and God. That's more or less your "triumph of love." I do not like the hysteria of Christianity but the broad and natural, working and building on all that been done by mankind, just a natural patterning of events. (KMM 47 BHP 40)

I was attracted to Marxism precisely because of the general sense of concern for "the oppressed." But I was also troubled by the Marxist/communist states that didn't give a damn about anyone. And I was desperate to be an atheist because God just didn't make sense to me.

November 5, 1979, letter to Mona Pehle

I have often felt that there were several thousand things wrong with Christianity and the doctrine of the Saviour is one of them. Christianity was at one stage a big power establishment and things may have been written into it as time went by. (KMM 34 BHP 127)

Reading through these extracts makes at least one thing clear. Already in 1964, well before her first hospitalization for a nervous breakdown, Head was thinking deeply about the nature of God and of evil. Marxist denials of God were limited because they defined the limits of a human life in material terms, scarcely capturing the harmony and beauty in human life that is expressed through love. She liked people, including Jesus Christ, and she specifically liked his humanity, even if she could not always understand what he stood for. Already, early on in her thought, God was in human beings, like Fantisi, who loved everyone without qualification. She accused Christianity of allowing people to abdicate responsibility for their own behavior, because they pray to a remote being who "has nothing to do with" them. "All should be Christ," and we should worship each other.

Head believed that evil would destroy itself. The significance of the battles in *A Question of Power* thus becomes clear. Elizabeth's battle for survival means that she must battle the evil in herself, not just in Dan, in order to survive. Like Elizabeth, we are all faced with a choice of good and evil, and this choice is made difficult because evil uses illusion (a concept from Buddhism)—like the busy, roaring highway of life. The dusty path that leads away from self-importance is not an illusion, but is more difficult.

And, as always, we must remember that John Mbiti's *African Religions and Philosophy* was important to the way Head conceptualized her vision. Many of his ideas resonate here: God in human life, the importance of love, the inevitability of evil and the fact of the choice we must make.

But Head also looked to the future. According to Mbiti, traditional religions are concerned with present and past time. Present time refers to the lifetime of an individual. The past refers to the lifetime of the community: "A person experiences time partly in his own individual life, and partly through the society which goes back many generations before his own birth" (17). God explains human contact with time (5) because God exists in both the past and the present; He is both transcendent and immanent (29). The past is important because it informs our decisions in the present. The past is not a finite concept, closed off as each moment passes. All people expect that eventually they will become part of it and assume that their present contributes to the collective past.

These concepts of past and present are important for understanding how Bessie Head altered the nature and purpose of her own experiences to make them Elizabeth's experiences in *A Question of Power* especially, but also in the imagined utopias of *When Rain Clouds Gather* and *Maru*. In her novels, Head explores time in ways that look forward to the future rather than back to the past. Elizabeth learns to understand her place in the present by examining her past, but she then uses that knowledge to reject power and to imagine a different future. Mbiti focused almost exclusively on the past and the present and how these inform the decisions that a community makes; thus certain patterns that were worked out in the past remain in place in the present—this is culture.

But Bessie Head saw the possibilities of learning from the past in order to break free of its grip. She studied history seriously, including unpublished dissertations, and corresponded with local historians in order to understand not just the events but also the patterns, principles, and forces of history.[12] About *Maru*, she wrote to Naomi Mitchison, "It is history for the future. It creates a new world. Your books put together the past, which I am not so good at but it will help me much—THE AFRICANS—when I want to figure out a link from there to something new" (KMM 331 BHP 3, July 18, 1970). Bessie Head was always looking forward. Ten years later, recounting a talk she gave in Gaborone, she wrote to Mona Pehle, "I gave an example of Chinua Achebe's early novels which could be considered historical novels and a recreation of Africa's past. I contrasted this with my own work which could be said to be a creation of the future" (KMM 34 BHP 151, June 3, 1980).

Dorothy Driver, in her review of Head's letters to Randolph Vigne, expressed Head's achievement and philosophy in terms of the power of ordinary events: "In a fascinating way the letters suggest, with their hints and repetitions, that the individual *is* the universe, and then, more specifically, that the individual is a historical manifestation of universal or elemental forces as well as of the unequal power structures of everyday life (colonial rule, chiefly authority, male domination and so on)" (17). Elizabeth's emotional and intellectual experience reflects the universality of the human experience: in the religious and cultural images that predominate in her vision, Elizabeth relives the oppression of apartheid and racism, which Sello then generalizes for her by bringing the poor of the world onto her bed (31).[13] But rather than "reconstructing history," as Driver goes on to

---

12  See also *Serowe: Village of the Rain Wind* and *A Bewitched Crossroad*.

13  Two other African theologians also offer insight into other ambiguities that appear in *A Question of Power*. Gabriel Setiloane's discussion of spirit possession among the Sotho-Tswana noted that in Sotho-Tswana societies, *go thwasa* refers to the condition of being possessed by a spirit. (In SePedi and SeRolong, *go thwasa* refers to the rituals necessary to become a *sangoma*/diviner/*ngaka*. In SePedi, *go thwathwaša* is to hatch; *go thwaša* is to be reborn. In SeSotho, *ho thoasa* also means to become renewed.) Setiloane reported that a person so possessed by a spirit usually behaves like a mad person and shuns company, like Elizabeth and Makhaya. However, *go thwasa* also means to come alive, and Setiloane suggested that this expression is used "because often this behaviour presages (or precedes) the recognition of the possession of a 'great Gift' in this person" (205), like Margaret. Traditionally, such a person would become a diviner or a seer, but Setiloane also cited reports of Christianized people who have experienced their calling by *go thwasa* (205–6). One need only think of many of the new African Christian churches, which encourage some form of possession among their practitioners.

Obed Kealotswe explained the role of African Independent Churches (AICs) in Botswana society; this role would probably have been clear to Bessie Head when she lived in Serowe. Kealotswe identified two aspects of the importance of AICs in Botswana: first, their influence on prophesy and witch-hunting, and second, their attention to the care of the poor and neglected (80).

suggest, Head wanted to "reconstruct" the future, that is, to imagine it very differently, and not just as an organic, logical extension of the past and present.

In Head's fiction, good and evil oppose one another, but they also exist together in the world, whether in a single entity like Elizabeth or in a more general social setting like Motabeng. The problem could be better expressed in terms of the difficulty of asserting good when one has knowledge of evil. How can good be affirmed when one has seen—and been—evil? Mbiti cites an example of an Ashanti priest who said that "'God has created the knowledge of good and evil in every person and allowed him to choose his way'" (199).[14] Understanding evil requires understanding the consequences and repercussions of an action, and this is what Bessie Head was very interested in: "Some people are going to be wiped out and killed, not by God but by the burden of their own evil destiny" (KMM 43 BHP 2, September 7, 1968, to Jean Highland). The ambiguous qualities of all the life forces and life forms reinforce the notion that evil is an inevitable part of life.

Writing in "Social and Political Pressures," Head said of *A Question of Power*, "I argued that people and nations do not realise the point at which they become evil; but once trapped in its net, evil has a powerful propelling motion into a terrible abyss of destruction. I argued that its form, design, and plan could be clearly outlined and that it was little understood as a force in the affairs of mankind" (69). Later, in "Notes from a Quiet Backwater II," she wrote that "I perceived the ease with which one could become evil and I associated evil in my mind with the acquisition of power" (77).[15] For Bessie Head herself,

---

Through these two functions, said Kealotswe, the AICs challenged the power of the chiefs, who assisted, and were supported by, different missionary organizations (81). The AICs offer a direct appeal to the Bible for answers, and this type of religious independence presented a threat to the traditional chiefs, to the London Missionary Society officials, and not least to the government (83). The prophet of an AIC attracts displaced people, especially women, who go to him for assistance with, for example, domestic violence and other social problems. In their affinity and concern for such displaced people, the AICs resemble in no small measure the kind of characters that Bessie Head drew in her novels: Makhaya and Gilbert, Maru, and Elizabeth and Sello.

14  See also Deut. 30:15 and 19: "See, I set before you today life and prosperity, death and destruction"; "This day I call heaven and earth as witnesses against you that I have set before you life and death, blessings and curses. Now choose life, so that you and your children may live."

15  Her statement is also reminiscent of the phrase "banality of evil," first coined by Hannah Arendt in 1963 to explain the complicity of ordinary people in making possible the rise of Nazism and the Holocaust—ordinary people who claimed to be only doing their duty.

the answer is a total rejection of power, both necessary and also extremely difficult, even perhaps impossible.

So, who is Bessie Head's God? Here again (1964–73) are her answers.

July 28, 1964, to Patrick Cullinan

God is wild and mad and illogical but He lets loose a thunderbolt in the most unexpected ways. There is this terrible unwritten law that nothing that is good and great has ever been handed to anyone on a plate. It is usually obtained through immense suffering. That's why I believe in Israel. God, really, is nothing clear to me and never will be, but people are. (*Imaginative Trespasser* 20)

June 11, 1969, to Randolph Vigne

People brought up on Christianity think God has nothing to do with them. He is someone who turns water into wine. They just go on shitting up the world and feel no responsibility for their character or anything they do. (*A Gesture of Belonging* 91)

January 16, 1971, to Randolph Vigne

I don't know how long it's been going on but I think I can say, with authority, that God in the end, is not an old man in the sky or invisible, but certain living individuals whom I adore. (*A Gesture of Belonging* 135)

July 15, 1971, to Randolph Vigne

For one brief moment I threw myself on the ground and said: "God, help me." Then I made an error. In the same breath I said: "Which God?" (*A Gesture of Belonging* 143)

August 13, 1971, to Randolph Vigne

We were still talking about God and church when I went to the loony bin. You said: "Be still and know that I am God." God is such a vague proposition in the heat of living and so often when I look back on what has been said, God seems to me to be the personality of individuals. (*A Gesture of Belonging* 148)

I wish the unknown God could walk in on me sometime, unexpectedly and say: "Here I am. Now love me." (*A Gesture of Belonging* 148)[16]

---

16 Possibly Head is also referring to the "Unknown God" in the Acts of the Apostles (17:22–24): "Paul then stood up in the meeting of the Areopagus and said: 'Men of Athens! I see that in every way you are very religious. For as I walked round and looked carefully at your objects of worship, I even found an altar with this inscription: TO AN UNKNOWN GOD. Now what you worship as something unknown I am going to proclaim to you."

I was baffled and tortured by this because on the one hand I could clearly feel that love wasn't only sex. It was force, food, life, mystery, heaven, the universe and wild flowers that unexpectedly grow with the spring rain and out of all that was created the infinite, the eternal AND GOD. (*A Gesture of Belonging* 149–50)[17]

August 21, 1973, to Giles Gordon (regarding Tolstoy's *Anna Karenina*)

But God, a big blind, broad concept, is carefully inserted at the most tragic moments. (KMM 44 BHP 43)

December 11, 1973, to Myrna Mackenzie

I think half of the anxieties left in me is that I became so thoroughly scared, I lost a lot of certainties—that there is a Good God looking very earnestly after man; that nothing could basically harm one. All that was lost and I realized how much of my life had been based on these sorts of assumptions and in reality, how ALONE each person is with a vast riddle, about life, about death. (KMM 23 BHP 49)

In these writings, the role of love in understanding the nature of God becomes more clear. These excerpts cover God's immanence, as well as his transcendence, and the importance, again of the moral choice between good and evil.

And they seem to suggest that love is God, and not the other way around.[18] To start with God is to immediately put it from you as something outside of you: "Writing for me depends on love, all physical reality depends on love but always it is an effort of will to create it. Simply because it is the one thing that cannot be created alone. It comes from outside" (September 15, 1965, *Imaginative Trespasser* 66). Love begins from within us but moves beyond us, to the outside, and near, in our neighbors, and so Head suggests that we do not come to love through God, but rather that we come to God through love, upon which "all physical reality depends." Bessie Head is asking us to look within

17 Craig MacKenzie writes that Head's "language and imagery . . . is germane to the world of the religious ascetic," and then that *Power*'s "argument . . . is that we have to renounce carnal love and other human passions" (154). But I think that Head's statement here refutes MacKenzie's, and thus she again makes contradictory understandings available to her readers.
18 Again, when I was growing up in the 1960s and 1970s, the phrase "God is Love" was very widespread, but it was being used (as I understood it) to draw people to God as a way of understanding how to love. It struck me as a very simplistic view of how to understand God: if you just believe in God, you'll love everything. But what I saw around me did not support that approach.

ourselves to find love, not just for ourselves, which is an empty love, but for others and in others.

In the letter to Myrna Mackenzie quoted above, Bessie Head wrote about having "lost a lot of certainties," alluding to the end of *When Rain Clouds Gather*. But already at the beginning of her first published novel, Head addresses the possibility that good and evil work in relationship. Dinorego, when he first meets Makhaya, explains the situation thus: " 'In this world are born both evil and good men. Both have to do justice to their cause' " (24). The reminder of our commonality comes also from Mma-Millipede: " 'Whether good or bad, each man is helpless before life' " (148). Life and death together form a pattern into which fit both good and evil: this is the sin and fate of all human beings. Each can choose to do good or evil, but we all must live in order to die.

Makhaya recognizes this common humanity when he meets Matenge for the first time: "[O]ne look at the face of Matenge instantly aroused his sympathy. It was the face of a tortured man, slowly being devoured by the intensity of his inner life . . . Being himself a lonely man, Makhaya instinctively sensed this" (69). Later, when he looks on Matenge's body in death, "a twisted spasm of pain swept across his face. Could the man hang like that with all the villagers staring in?" (203). In Golema Mmidi, he comes face to face with a kind of evil he recognizes in the figure of a person he feels sympathy for. Still later, the familiarity he feels when he sees Matenge is recast and magnified when he learns love because of death. He only admits love for Paulina when he realizes that she will have to face the horror of her son's death in the bush: "What sort of man was he who only gave way to love under extreme pressure and pain? . . . If he loved Paulina now and admitted it to himself, it was because he sensed that she might be facing tragedy, and that she could not face it alone" (178–79). Once he admits his love, he is living Dinorego's and Mma-Millipede's pronouncements that both good and evil must face death and life—both the little boy and Chief Matenge die, and he and Paulina live.

Olaussen believes that in fact Makhaya becomes God for Paulina, since she turns to him (rather than to Him) when her son fails to return from the cattle post (258). Lauren Smith states that the "Good God" has the last word at the end of *When Rain Clouds Gather*, when He states His intent to revenge himself on Makhaya (64). But some of the last paragraphs of the novel suggest a more intricate prospect.

Makhaya comes to live within the complexity of paradox, but Dinorego's "Good God" is still too far away, still too powerful, watching the events unfold in the village, but planning the best for "all his favourite people" so that they can "show everyone else just how quickly things could really change":

> But why were they all so boring this evening? Ah, but he was a little bored too. His favourite mouthpiece, Dinorego, was away at the funeral.
>
> Therefore the Good God cast one last look at Makhaya, whom he intended revenging almightily for his silent threat to knock him down. He would so much entangle this stupid young man with marriage and babies and children that he would always have to think, not twice but several hundred times, before he came to knocking anyone down.
>
> He wandered along the footpath, in the direction of the sunset, and stopped for a while in the yard of Paulina Sebeso. She was busy at her smoke haze fire, preparing supper, but she paused and looked up expectantly as she heard familiar footsteps. It was Makhaya coming home. (214–15)

The "He" that opens the final paragraph is almost impossibly ambiguous, and the ambiguity between Makhaya and the Good God is striking in terms of Bessie Head's developing ideas. Some have identified it as an error of editing, but the evidence in that paragraph itself does not entirely support this belief.[19] "He" stops for a while in Paulina's yard, but she does not look up until she hears familiar footsteps, those of Makhaya, who is "coming home" and therefore apparently not already in the yard. At the very least, God and Makhaya are walking the same path.

As readers, interacting with the narrator, and the writer, we are also pulled into the chain of thoughts by the first three sentences of the quotation: the first one is actually a question, answered by the second two sentences in the mind of the speaker. We are informed by the narrator, who is created by the writer. Who is Dinorego? Who is God? Who is Bessie Head? Who am I? Head's question, "Which God?" (quoted above), becomes very personal, and not just for Bessie Head.

---

19  Furthermore, all extant drafts and editions of *When Rain Clouds Gather* preserve this "He."

Olaussen also notes, "Head's identification of Makhaya with God is further developed in the two following novels" (164). She quotes from a letter,[20]

> The hero Makhaya, whom I used as my spokesman, is brought to a crossroad. He looks both ways. One road leads to fame and importance. He chooses: I shall take the road that leads to peace of mind. I shall choose a quiet backwater and work together with people. They were the choices of a God. The word God then leaps to the fore in the next two books. (qtd. in Olaussen 164)

This footpath appears again in *Maru*.[21]

Like Makhaya, Maru is also searching for goodness. He is a more complicated figure than Makhaya, however, and Head lamented that "[a]s for Maru he was swallowed whole, only one reviewer pointing out that he is really a combination of good and evil" (KMM 24 BHP 34, January 22, 1972, to Giles Gordon). Maru carries a picture in his heart of a choice that he realizes he must face: "There was a busy, roaring highway on one side, full of bustle and traffic. Leading away from it was a small, dusty footpath. It went on and on by itself into the distance" (274). Maru has always hesitated to take the dusty path, even though the gods in his heart have told him to follow it, because he sees no companion to walk it with him. After Margaret arrives, however, the path is edged with bright yellow daisies that dance in the sunlight; "The sight was so beautiful that his heart leapt with joy" (274). He recognizes that Margaret will be his companion.

The nature of the choice that Maru sees in his heart reflects the discrepancy that he sees in the village. Maru "set the tone, seemingly, for a new world" (261), but he cannot do it alone. In *Maru*, the extremes cannot be reconciled to one another: Maru cannot marry Margaret and still remain in Dilepe in part because he understands that he is "not a living dynamo . . . He, Maru, was the dreamer of this *future* greatness" (278–79, my emphasis). Maru is a god for the future, not for the present, which he manipulates for his own dreams. And so

---

20  Identified as KMM 34 BHP 151, but I have been unable to find the quotation.
21  A practicing Catholic friend reminded me that the image of two paths is also a familiar Christian symbol.

he puts his capacity for cruelty to the service of his capacity for goodness and his dreams:

> [T]he motivation came from the gods who spoke to him in his heart. They had said: Take that road. Then they had said: Take that companion. He believed his heart and the things in it. They were his only criteria for goodness. In the end nothing was personal to him. In the end, the subjection of his whole life to his inner gods was an intellectual process. Very little feeling was involved. His methods were cold, calculating and ruthless. (282)

He is ultimately as ruthless as Pete, and the "intellectual process" is sterile and brutal. His love for Margaret and his dreams for justice also make him manipulative and cruel.

The representation of these contrasting visions of life, of other people, is carried throughout the novel, and the contradictory nature of Dilepe, of human cruelty and goodness, expresses itself individually in both Margaret and Maru. Maru faces the choice of the diverging paths, but Dikeledi notices as well that Margaret "was a shadow behind which lived another personality of great vigour and vitality . . . You were never sure whether she was greater than you, or inferior, because of this constant flux and inter-change between her two images" (279–80). Dikeledi notices that the two Margaret-images "constantly tripped up each other" (280). When the principal Pete tries to engineer Margaret's dismissal, Dikeledi discovers that Margaret is also "very violent and dominant" but that she is "seemingly unable to project that hidden power" (280), despite the fact that a little girl puts her hand to her throat at the same time that Margaret thinks she is killing her.

Margaret and Dikeledi defeat Pete, and Margaret fulfills the prophecy of the elder Margaret, who promised that " 'One day you will help your people' " (231). So Margaret marries and is brought into "a living death" (329) for the sins of society. I am reminded of Christ's sacrifice for the sins of humanity. Marilyn Miller-Bagley noted Head's use of Christian imagery in describing Margaret's mother's death, suggesting that this imagery implies the "Messianic" role of Margaret (58–59): "she will ultimately take on the racial sins of those around her" (50). But Margaret's burden is in fact a twofold one: it is a task she must undertake in aid of social justice, and it is an emotional burden because in order to take it on, she must leave two people she loves. Maru's personality encompasses the same kind of dichotomy—the same double nature—that Margaret displays. His plans are not personal because they involve social change, but his choices reflect an intense desire for personal happiness, even if that happiness comes at someone else's, that is, Margaret's, expense.

Sello's definition of love and Elizabeth's relationships with the people of the co-op contrast sharply with Dan's love, which "was exclusive, between her and him alone" (117). Sello rescues her when he says, "'Elizabeth, love isn't like that. Love is two people mutually feeding each other, not one living on the soul of the other like a ghoul!'" (197). But love is also many people, more than two, "feeding" each other. The marriages of *When Rain Clouds Gather* and *Maru* represent the assumption of an outsider into a community, but the couple remains always beyond the community: walking off together into the bush or living in exile in a remote spot. In a 1969 letter (October 16) to Paddy Kitchen, Head wrote that "I have found that a love as found between married people must be honourable if others are to be included and allowed to walk in and out of the door" (KMM 74 BHP 4).[22] Elizabeth's integration into Motabeng reflects that ideal—she and Sello "had perfected together the ideal of sharing everything and then perfectly shared everything with all mankind" (202)—but it is also different because at the end she is, perhaps necessarily, alone.

Margaret experiences a kind of foreshadowing of her future when she paints Maru's dreams, which he sends her. She describes a dream in which she sees

"two people embrace each other . . . I felt so ashamed, thinking I had come upon a secret which ought not to be disclosed, that I turned and tried to run away. Just then a strong wind arose and began to blow me in the direction of the embracing couple. I was terrified. They did not want anyone near them and I could feel it." (310)

This vision anticipates her marriage to Maru, both her relationship with him and her isolation from Moleka and Dikeledi, but it also echoes the walk that Gilbert and Maria take into the bush on their wedding day in *When Rain Clouds Gather*, and it anticipates the vision of two lovers that Dan shows Elizabeth.

---

22  But at the same time, she was apparently incapable of writing such a marriage.

Gilbert and Maria, and Margaret and Maru, exist separately from others; only Sello suggests that love is different. Elizabeth, in contrast to Makhaya and Margaret, does not marry, whether to remain in Motabeng or not.

If Maru is a god, then he is removed from his people, and what kind of god does that make him? Not the kind Bessie Head likes, as Elizabeth concludes at the end of *A Question of Power*. Maru's marriage to an outcast points up a social injustice, but the gossip in Dilepe leaves them socially dead, although we are told that "a door silently opened on the small, dark airless room in which [the San's] souls had been shut for a long time. The wind of freedom . . . turned and flowed into the room" (331). (This statement contributes to the sense of "unresolvability" that for me permeates the end of the novel.) Maru's and Margaret's marriage illustrates the extreme possibilities present in the marriages of Gilbert and Maria, Makhaya and Paulina: marriage to one person excludes others.

In 1978, Bessie Head wrote that "I found myself in a situation where there was no guarantee against the possibility that I could be evil too" ("Some Notes on Novel Writing" 63).[23] *A Question of Power* explores the contradictory, ambiguous, irreconcilable, impossible nature of the human character, a question that both *When Rain Clouds Gather* and *Maru* raise. In the same essay ("Some Notes on Novel Writing"), Head wrote that "[i]t was necessary for me to concentrate directly on people because I believe it is only people who make people suffer and not some hidden, unknown God or devil" (63). Elizabeth, an underdog from a cruel and oppressive society, is the medium for the exploration, and in her suffering, she wanders freely into and out of questions regarding the nature of cruelty, God, love, sex, racism, identity, perfection, community, friendship, and cooperation. For Elizabeth in *A Question of Power*, embracing the "brotherhood of man" means loving "the GOD IN ALL MEN" (KMM 43 BHP 2, September 7, 1968, to Jean Highland).

---

23 In 1964, in "Where Is the Hour of the Beautiful Dancing of Birds in the Sun-Wind," Head wrote of her experience of love (whether of a single man or of all "men" is unclear, of course), "I want something to share the blame because I am stark-terrified at what I may be driven to do. You see, the last card I hold, face down—its name is power too. Not anything you may care to understand; being odd, personal, withdrawn, it is all of my own fashioning. Still, it bears the same stamp of the thing men use against each other in the pursuit of ambition" (156).

Many of these issues, introduced in Head's previous work, are explored in *A Question of Power* with an almost unparalleled ferocity. Head's conclusions regarding the way to human happiness and fulfillment are certainly idealistic in their characterization: "the land" which Elizabeth claims at the end of *A Question of Power* is in many ways the Garden of Eden, but the conclusion embraces the whole of human experience, both good and evil, and affirms the possibility—but not the inevitability—of good.

In fact, Elizabeth can be God because of, not in spite of, the qualities that make her human:

> [T]he basic error seemed to be a relegation of all things holy to some unseen Being in the sky. Since man was not holy to man, he could be tortured for his complexion, he could be misused, degraded and killed. If there were any revelation whatsoever in her own suffering it seemed to be quite the reverse of Mohammed's dramatic statement. He had said: There is only one God and his name is Allah. And Mohammed is his prophet.
>
> She said: There is only one God and his name is Man. And Elizabeth is his prophet. (205–6)

Ultimately, Elizabeth finds a way to live with all the manifestations of God because what is common to all the gods and to all her experiences of history and culture is herself, the human being Elizabeth. This intimate communion between divinity and humanity characterizes many concepts of many religions, and it acknowledges the historical and social forces that shape human beings. These forces are past and present, good and evil, and because they are always present, this process is possibly an unending one.

This intimate relationship between good, evil, and power is personified in the characters of Dan and Sello. Here, Bessie Head describes them.

April 1, 1972, to Giles Gordon

Sello is the Makhaya-type man of my other two books. He is far worse off than the elusive, sensitive Makhaya who was at least alive and the complicated Maru. He is the peak development of those two men but so complex and yet I feel possibly, my top achievement so far. The Sello in the book is not flesh and blood, yet he is; there are indications that he is alive—they are almost incidental. The full concentration is on his soul. (KMM 24 BHP 35)

<u>September 19, 1972, to Daphne Ehrlich (Houghton Mifflin)</u>

God and the devil are presented as running mates but what upsets people is that God is presented as a man with normal human fallibility, plus conscience, while the devil is conscienceless evil. The fallible, human and conscience is all that saves God, while it is clearly shown that the devil has no need for these qualities.

The man Sello in the story represents this version of God but more, the power of him is a past, long long ago of degradation on which he builds the monastic ideal of restraint, sacrifice and service—that is, the man's eventual perfection is based on what he did in his depths. He re-lives the degradation only as a teaching for Elizabeth. (KMM 107 BHP 1)

Dan is just evil. Sello is not alive, but he is, and in his being alive he has all the complications and contradictions of a human being. He has also lived through many lives and been reborn many times and "had the long history of the human race in his heart, as he was Old Father Time" (201). Perhaps he is the single figure who embodies God, but who is only representative, because love is possible in everyone.

Sello arrives first, and early in their relationship he tells her that " '[i]t is when you cry, in the blackest hour of despair, that you stumble on a source of goodness' " (34). His statement is a kind of premonition for Elizabeth, because it encompasses the lesson she must learn about the nature of the human soul. Sello says, " 'Everything was evil until I broke down and cried . . . Then we said: "Send us perfection." They sent you. Then we asked: "What is perfection?" And they said: "Love." ' " (34). If Elizabeth is to survive, she must understand what Sello's statements mean for her: "What is love? Who is God? If I cry, who will have compassion on me as my suffering is the suffering of others? This is the nature of evil. This is the nature of goodness" (70). These questions that Elizabeth poses for herself are profoundly spiritual, but when it is all over, Elizabeth has "no illusions left about God or mercy or pity. A victim simply stared in the face of evil, and died" (200). A victim gives up on love, gives up responsibility for the self. Elizabeth learns to give and, perhaps more importantly for her inner peace, to accept love, to feed and to be fed. Elizabeth's answers come from herself and from the people with whom she works and lives. The experience of breakdown is a solitary one, and it is hellish, because

Hell, for Elizabeth, is a lack of community and can only be counteracted by "the presence of love" (Olaussen 69).

Elizabeth's questions about good, evil, love, and God are answered in the activities of the co-op, a kind of a new garden. Jean Marquard wrote that "the ideal garden is once again cultivated on a co-operative basis" (60), recalling Voltaire's *Candide*, and indeed Elizabeth flees to it from the political life of South Africa. But Elizabeth's actions are no longer the passive actions of someone who just wants to be left alone. Elizabeth is not just hiding from her past; she turns away from the oppressive behavior she learned in South Africa and toward a new way of life, one in which the personal qualities of political life are acknowledged in the organization of the spiritual "brotherhood of man."[24] The co-op is also a secular Garden of Eden. Its activities represent a world where human beings have not yet lost their holiness to the corrupt ethics of an oppressive power, but it is also a world where the Fall is not possible because human beings already have knowledge of good and evil and are the only God. When Elizabeth tries to apologize to Eugene, he stops her and affirms his faith in her: "He was that kind of man. People were always going up and up and up, never down and down and down" (204). Head even refers to him as "the Eugene man," a possible allusion to his participation in corporate humanity as an aspect of God.

This world seems infinitely preferable to the world presented in Lessing's *The Grass Is Singing.* Twenty years ago, I read Lessing's novel alongside *A Question of Power.* I still think they can be read alongside each other, if only as a reminder to work towards a more hopeful future, rather than succumbing to the despair that pervades *The Grass Is Singing*—a novel I nevertheless like.

The characters in *A Question of Power* redeem themselves.[25] Mary Turner's world in *The Grass Is Singing* offers no such redemption. There is no Garden of Eden; there is only the failing farm in the hot, dry, endless bush, with its shrilling cicadas. There is no sense of community, only the isolation that Mary feels. Mary has no sense of purpose, but she does have a sense of her own

---

24 The personal, ordinary nature of the political world is a topic that Head explores in more detail in her subsequent work, *Serowe: Village of the Rain Wind* (1981) and *A Bewitched Crossroad* (1984). See also Dorothy Driver's review of the Vigne correspondence.

25 Even the evil Camilla is made to recognize her racist attitudes: Elizabeth "met a totally changed woman with a soft, subdued air, as near as a woman of her type could ever come to brooding reflection" (86).

destiny, represented especially by the store, which represents the isolation and the hopelessness of her childhood. It was "the center of her life" (29), where she spent time "looking covertly at the little Greek girl whom she was not allowed to play with because her mother said her parents were dagoes" (30). It was also the symbol of poverty, the "powerful, implacable place that sent in bills at the end of the month" (31). Once the store fails, it becomes the abandoned temple of her past, a past that keeps intruding into her life to prevent any change.

Elizabeth's spiritual experiences enable her incorporation into Motabeng: Sello begins his work by introducing her to people *and* by appearing as a monk;[26] Tom, Eugene, and Kenosi draw her into the activities of the co-op. (This work is what Desiree Lewis called the integration of the corporeal and the spiritual.) When her soul-death ends, it ends twice: once, "though she did not realize it," when Tom (in the tradition of Advaita Vedanta) broadens the circle of love to include vegetables (188), and again and finally when Sello redefines love (197). Both Sello's and Tom's insights are critical for Elizabeth's emerging vision. The vision has secular aspects, described by the co-op and the people (and vegetables) there, but the spirituality that Sello offers is equally important.

At the end of *A Question of Power*, Elizabeth celebrates the human spirit in its ordinary manifestation, not in a supreme being or in the powers of the living-dead:

> "It was Sello. It seemed to me that his job was religion itself, because he moved towards me like that, then right in front of my eyes did a slow, spiritual strip-tease act. He half showed me that the source of human suffering was God itself, personalities in possession of powers or energies of the soul. Ordinary people never mucked up the universe. They don't have that kind of power, wild and flaring out of proportion. They have been the victims of it . . ." (190, ellipsis in original)

Hers is a corporate God, but God is also corporate humanity.

---

26  Sello and Elizabeth also travel together as monks: "Maybe, the work she and Sello had done together had introduced a softness and tenderness into mankind's history. The flowers, the animals, the everyday events of people's lives had been exalted by them. They had roamed the world together as barefoot monks, and eaten strange food to sustain them through their monastic disciplines" (202).

In "African Religions," Head wrote of Mbiti's work, "Professor Mbiti, in his quiet and detached interpretations of African religions, side-steps the snobs and explains the way of life of a mass of people who were for so long discounted in the scheme of things" (51). Head rejected the relationship of power and reorganized the elements of her spiritual education to create a more cosmopolitan vision that serves—and enhances—the community of the faithful. Rukmini Vanamali alludes to the change: Sello "had accumulated a vast store or experience and knowledge in that sphere; *a similar background of evolving religious consciousness is postulated for Elizabeth.* The belief in the doctrine of rebirth must be understood as central to Bessie Head's metaphysics. She makes a *profession of faith* in her Address for the University of Calabar seminar" (159, my emphasis).[27] Once again Head attests to the commonality of experience (of both good and evil) and the potential for change that Elizabeth personifies. Head's profession of faith found its ultimate expression in Elizabeth and Sello, whose spiritual consciousness encompasses the whole of human experience and whose prophecy places Elizabeth at the service of humankind, in the incarnation of Motabeng. Head's vision entails recognizing both the value of the individual in the community and the value of that community. The two cannot be separated. The way the life is lived collectively defines the quality of the individual, spiritual life. Head's vision, Elizabeth's prophecy, expresses the hope that each person's unique contribution will be esteemed but that individuality will not become an excuse to acquire power—because we are all God.

As I was finishing this chapter, I began yet again to think again about what I believe. I was nominally—perhaps the word is vaguely—raised in the Roman Catholic faith, so my perspective here has been necessarily, nominally, vaguely, Christian. But by the time I was twenty-one, I had stopped going to Mass completely. I was proud to announce myself an atheist, but I am not sure that I was. It was fashionable, of course—I was going through a period when Marxism appealed to me strongly; it was also important to demonstrate that I did not simply follow in my "capitalistic" parents' footsteps. Of course,

---

27 In the passage Vanamali quotes, Head describes her view on reincarnation, arguing that each individual is an accumulation of knowledge from past lives, and she also spoke about her own life.

I never asked them what they believed in. I never had that sort of conversation with my mother, and I have only recently begun to talk about such things with my father, who finally asked me one day, "Do you believe in God?"

Do I believe in God? I cannot say. I do not believe in the God of my childhood, although I still find myself looking up and whispering bargains into the void. Most clearly I remember trying to strike some kind of bargain when my mother died: I promised to sleep kneeling by the side of her bed forever if she recovered, all the while wondering who I was trying to plead with. She did not, of course, recover. It does not work like that. Yet still I find myself whispering into the void.

So apparently I believe something. When I was working on the original dissertation, I became aware that my attitude towards God and all things spiritual was undergoing a profound change. I could no longer glibly state that I was an atheist. There was something in Bessie Head, something very moving, that I could not put my hands on, but I kept returning to the same phrases: *Help me. Sello is both God and the Devil at the same time. Who will have pity on me as my suffering is the suffering of others? It was Makhaya coming home.* There was no other way to explain the genius of sentences like those I was reading or the fact that they were having such a profound effect on me that I wanted to find God.

And now, as I rewrite all these ideas and think about the person I was then, I ask myself the same question. I still do not know. I do know that I am attracted to people of deep faith, no matter how that faith is expressed. I think that Bessie Head was a person of deep faith.

And I think there is something that sets human beings apart. I once tried to do a writing exercise in which I had to describe a person I loved. Somehow, I found myself instead listing all the people I love. I went back to that list after my mother died, because she was, I think, a person who loved indiscriminately, like Fantisi. She scolded us when we said we hated someone: "You don't hate them. You just dislike their ways." One of her best friends maintained that my mother had such a strong sense of right and wrong that she did not worry most of the time if someone disagreed with her. So when I went back to my list, I wondered if it did not crystallize something for me that my mother had, very quietly, been teaching me my whole life. How do you love a person? You just do. That is why we are here. Because otherwise, why would we love?

But I must give Bessie the last word.

> What Africa has, what is significant, is that the top most, the greatest of these heroes, were born with black skins. Then, for my personal experience, I got attached to some white people, also, the inner part was gigantic. They were the lovely dreams I mentioned to you before. They used to straight away appear in dreams as the identical replica of myself. One woman, my exact reproduction said touchingly: "What must I now call myself, Coloured or Negro?" as though puzzled by having suddenly been faced with a strange situation. I looked at the soul volume in the dream. It was twice my size, she was so big and great. As I looked at her, she hastily placed something in front of her and said: "I prefer to be your equal."
>
> The range of such people, for the new age, is equally distributed for all nations but the fierce balance of good and evil is really fought for the black man in Africa and America and he is the only race who has the choice: "ALL THIS I'LL GIVE YOU IF YOU WILL <u>BOW</u> DOWN and worship me." The most fearful demons from the darkest pits of hell want him but the greatest Gods who give love and service freely are also available to him.[28]
>
> What I really came to look on with sheer dread was the person referred to as "the King" . . . You don't know what to make of him because he is half perfection, and when that shows, it glitters beyond the brightest diamond. The other side of him, wrecked universe after universe. I tentatively saw it as the wrong version of love, a mixture of self-importance and a love for slaves. The self-importance destroys love which is a touchy thing.
>
> (KMM 74 BHP 20, May 26, 1970, to Paddy Kitchen)

---

28 The quotation in this paragraph is from Mt. 4:9, the temptation of Jesus by Satan in the desert. Satan offers him all the kingdoms of the world if Jesus will "bow down and worship" him.

# 6

# Rereading Bessie Head

*I have spoke with the tongue of angels*
*I have held the hand of a devil*
*It was warm in the night*
*I was cold as a stone*
*But I still haven't found*
*What I'm looking for*

U2, "I Still Haven't Found What I'm Looking for"

In the opening chapter of this book, I noted that in *Living on a Horizon*, Desiree Lewis observed that Bessie Head's works "defy conclusive interpretation" (15). If this book has accomplished anything, I suppose—and indeed hope?—it is in proving the absolute truth of Lewis's observation. Someone who read these chapters mused, "I wonder if . . . it is necessary to take *partial* views." Then he reminded me of the story of the elephant and the blind men, who understood something different according to which part of the elephant they were touching—a tree trunk, a wall, a hose, a sword. Perhaps Bessie Head is like the elephant: each part offering something different and all the parts together creating something improbable but still inevitable. Eventually it becomes impossible to make a single, conclusive, summarizing statement about what she believed, what she thought, and what she means.

Of course, this is not an original idea. It is perhaps a truism that great literature offers something new to its readers each time they read it. But Lewis made another statement about Bessie Head that I think identifies what makes her work almost (but not quite) unique. In "Bessie Head's Freedoms," Lewis wrote that "Head is read in terms of what the reader would like to see," suggesting that criticism appropriates for its own purposes and ideologies only particular aspects of Head's writing. To some extent, I think this is true, but I also believe that reading Bessie Head in terms of what we want to see is not necessarily a bad thing, and that in fact Bessie Head encourages it because of her interest in engaging those who read her: her correspondence contains hundreds of letters from people who knew her only through her writing. This is not the "appropriating impulse" of literary criticism that Lewis identifies, but instead a deeply personal assessment of one's own self in the engagement with literature. When I read her, I see what I want to see because of who I am at the time, but because I also change, Bessie Head changes me and then changes with me, so that when I reread, we are always different. Peter Carlton describes a similar experience of rereading *Middlemarch*, comparing the experience to Dorothea's return to her boudoir after her marriage to Casaubon:

> Every rereading is like returning to a familiar room and finding it changed. I take the tiny backward step that brings me back home to myself, and I begin to look around, half-curious and half-fearful to discover who or what will emerge from the disenchanted background, gather new breath and meaning and tell me something about myself that I may or may not want to know. (238–39)

Dorothea, he writes, "cannot admit [her desire for Will Ladislaw, recalled to her in the boudoir] to herself, so she rejects it, just as I would like to reject some aspects of myself that come out to greet me every time I open my haunted copy of the novel" (239). So, too, I return to Bessie Head's writing, both with a yearning for something that eludes me and at the same time somewhat fearful that I will find it.

What I have tried to approach, if not exactly show, in the course of this book is a type of conversation that is very unusual in literature. (Unusual, but not unknown: *Shakespeare and I* describes a similar experience of "conversation" with Shakespeare's plays, and I will refer to this anthology later.) Because it is possible to agree and disagree with what she says, because she does not provide easy morals, because she makes blanket statements about all people (and all types of people), because she includes herself in her pronouncements and because she then also asserts that she is different, to really read Bessie Head—and not just put her aside—means that when we read her we are also agreeing, disagreeing, and challenging—we are conversing with her.

Head's characters are often responding to horrors that have occurred in their own lives. The struggle makes them both mad and utterly sane. They respond to the horrors of their pasts in recognizable ways, but we cannot dismiss them as completely mad because of the way their responses draw in other characters. The presumed sanity of those around them thus makes a blanket condemnation of insanity impossible: if outsiders experience what goes on in a character's head, then it is not just inside that one character's head, but is real, part of the reality of the text that we the readers must therefore also accept as real. Once we do that, we raise questions about the reality of our own thoughts and minds. When I read Bessie Head, this question is important to me because of my own anxieties about my life.

Whether we are born male or female has certain social implications, but those implications are not as important to our selves as is the question of whether and how we take responsibility for those around us. Do we enable those around us to flourish as human beings? For Bessie Head this question is central: male and female characters are described in terms of how well they take care of those who are in their charge. We can be men or women, but we must look out for others. Our sex is, in this central, crucial matter, irrelevant.

But I *am* a feminist: How do I interact with men? Am I responsible? Am I fair?

Our race is irrelevant, too. Bessie Head shows us how very similar we all are to one another by giving her characters unexpected qualities. Two white men make it possible for a black refugee to find a life in a small village, in spite of the hostility of its black chief. A paramount chief sets social change in motion by marrying an outcast who was raised by a white woman who instilled in her a sense of responsibility for her outcast people. A Coloured woman is tortured by a man who is characterized in terms of white stereotypes of black men but who also expresses himself in terms of African nationalist stereotypes about others. With whom are we to feel sympathy?

And me? A friend once asked her class to define "an African" and then asked them to explain how I am African, too. But I am American—and from the United States, not Canada, white, and not only in my skin color, which is ultimately irrelevant. Cultural whiteness is part of my background, my collective past, my cultural baggage. I am often afraid that I act like a white person, rather than like a human being, because of assumptions about others that I have not yet uncovered in myself. But as I try to define myself, the usual "signifiers" seem inappropriate, and I discover a similar sentiment expressed by Tim Brennan: "White authenticity has too often seemed to mean planting the flag of ethnicity squarely on the white page . . . My formative culture was crisscrossed not by ethnicity but by a web of arbitrary institutional possibilities" (181), possibilities that at the same time I recognize are often denied to others.[1]

Eventually, the physical becomes irrelevant, but at the same time it is the basis for all human interaction, given that we exist in the physical world, not only in the spiritual one. Bessie Head even refers to the physical world as the manifestation of love (letter of September 15, 1965, to Patrick Cullinan, *Imaginative Trespasser* 66). Marilynne Robinson wrote about this false separation: "There is a deeply rooted notion that the material exists in opposition to the spiritual, precludes or repels or trumps the sacred as an idea. This dichotomy goes back at least to the dualism of the Manichees, who believed the physical world was the creation of an evil god in perpetual conflict with a good god" ("Reclaiming a Sense of the Sacred"). In Bessie Head we are forced to confront this false dichotomy because her writing breaks down the false barriers between people: black/white, woman/man, foreigner/local, outsider/insider, and so on. We cannot slot her characters and the things that happen to them in predictable ways. We can only ask ourselves how these things happen in the novels, and consider how they happen in our lives.

This breaking down can be seen in the three novels in many aspects: in the way that the style moves from more realistic in *When Rain Clouds Gather* to more surreal in *A Question of Power*; in the way that the characters move from engagement with their communities to more introspection; in the way that the role of those same communities increases in importance from *When Clouds Gather* to *A Question of Power*, despite the fact that the communities themselves recede somewhat into the background (what Gillian Stead Eilersen called the inward movement of the trilogy); in the way that God becomes

---

1  William L. Andrews: "Just because I had made a gesture of solidarity didn't mean that the differences, whether of class or of color, that estrange us even from those with whom we feel a bond would simply relax and disappear" (247).

both more indistinct and more universal. Bessie Head wrote about the novels that they

> draw very heavily on autobiographical experience. I personally was concerned with power and how to evade it. This was based on a fear that African liberation was mainly a wild rush for power. African people need more than that from their leadership. There has to be broad planning for the people to solve centuries of poverty and exploitation. I tended to be caught in the intensity of this dialogue and for a long time, through all three novels, held on to the same theme. (KMM 186 BHP 45, November 25, 1977, to Margaret Walker Alexander)

During my work on this book, I have engaged with Bessie Head, but also with my friends and family, colleagues, other works of literature (some of which might seem like very odd choices that exist in out-of-the-way places or on the margins of "literature"), and with my own attitude toward my upbringing and toward my soul. Robinson also has the following to say about the soul:

> When I write fiction, I suppose my attempt is to simulate the integrative work of a mind perceiving and reflecting, drawing upon culture, memory, conscience, belief or assumption, circumstance, fear, and desire—a mind shaping the moment of experience and response and then reshaping them both as narrative . . .

> Modern discourse is not really comfortable with the word "soul," and in my opinion the loss of the word has been disabling, not only to religion but to literature and political thought and to every humane pursuit . . . So the soul, the masterpiece of creation, is more or less reduced to a token signifying cosmic acceptance or rejection, having little or nothing to do with that miraculous thing, the felt experience of life, except insofar as life offers distractions or temptations.

In the first chapter of this book, I wrote that I wanted to find out why reading Bessie Head has the effect on me that it does, and how reading her is a prolonged drawing-out of my own desires. The questions arise: What are my own desires? What moments and experiences in my life intersect with the emotional and intellectual activity of reading Bessie Head? What memories, beliefs, assumptions, and fears do I draw on that shape my ever-changing reaction to Bessie Head? I have tried to show some of them in the course of this book.

What I am finding and exploring, through Bessie Head's exploration of hers, is my own soul. I am now more convinced than ever that there is "something out there," although I am, like Head, both unwilling, given the preponderance of human suffering, and at the same time yearning to acknowledge the existence of something greater than myself. I discover the growing importance of love in my relationships with other people and my need to take care of them, but of course I am unable to quantify it. I want to do work that is meaningful in the sense that it contributes something positive to other people's lives and their sense of themselves, and I can quantify my work, but I cannot qualify its impact or effect.

As I was finishing the previous chapter, I read a notice about an anthology called *Shakespeare and I*, a collection of essays by Shakespeare scholars who wrote about their experience of working on Shakespeare and how the encounter with his plays offers ongoing opportunities for self-reflection and change. I bought it immediately. The editors, in their introduction, discuss how contemporary criticism lacks the capacity to foster and nourish this kind of personal engagement with literature. They cite Stephen Greenblatt: "'Literary criticism is on the whole almost unbearable to read because it lacks much in the way of personal stakes and commitment. The only way to get those qualities is to actually put yourself on the line as somebody' (Greenblatt, quoted in Blume, 2001)" (9). Their answer is their own anthology: "*Shakespeare and I* takes Greenblatt's advice seriously, perhaps even more seriously than Greenblatt himself does. This call for literary critics to hold on to and take responsibility for their individual 'voices' is only dimly and imperfectly heard in current criticism" (9). Their statement calls to mind earlier assertions by Ellen Messer-Davidow, and Candace Lang, and Frances Murphy Zauhar, that critics need to be aware of and define their own preconceptions, and that conventional criticism rewards detachment rather than engagement.

The editors of *Shakespeare and I* also refer to Montaigne's essays, taking issue with the claims of "egotism, arrogance and solipsism" often attributed to him:

> Yes, it is conceivable that the kind of criticism we are advocating and striving
> to practice could be seen as the mere Shakespearean extension or corollary

of a much wider and more pervasive contemporary culture of the self, a "me" culture that encompasses the aggressively competitive individualism of modern business, as well as the vapid narcissism of reality TV. For Montaigne, however, to "talk about yourself" and "to think about yourself" is not the sign of such vanity; it is its "sovereign remedy" (Montaigne, trans. Screech, 2003, p. 426). People must talk and think about themselves, Montaigne implies; otherwise they risk "fal[ling]" passively into "an injudicious self-love" (ibid.). (11)

That "injudicious self-love" is destructive; it does not eventually turn outward to find its reflection in others.

The editors are looking for the "pleasure-giving impact that reading and watching Shakespeare has on life" (14). That is exactly it. I, too, look for the "pleasure-giving impact" of literature: reading it, writing about it—I find it most strongly in Bessie Head[2] (but elsewhere, too, of course). And the first essay in the anthology offered me one explanation for my own fascination.

In "Mea Culpa," Ewan Fernie looks to Angelo in *Measure for Measure* to explain a part of himself to himself. He, too, begins his essay by questioning the place of objectivity in academic criticism: "it conditions our response . . . to the effect that scholarship is now a professional business largely sealed off from enthusiastic reading. It is hard for contemporary academic readers to do justice to the sheer life and life-potential of a book" (21). And here is Bessie Head again, but in Fernie's words: "I also believe . . . that another way of renewing an intense and serious intellectual engagement with art is via a new engagement with . . . the sort of theology that really connects up with the Big Stuff [life, death, meaning, value], nothing too pious, pompous or metaphysical" (22–23).

For Fernie, the issue is one of desire. Angelo, who commits rape at the end of the play, is a difficult character, because Fernie identifies with him in his desire: "For love itself—perhaps the last touchstone of humanist criticism—is

2 "*Power* is also highly innovative, though . . . it is radical in a way that goes beyond what modernism attempted with its stream-of-consciousness techniques and its psychological realism. *Power* abandons distinctions that fundamentally structure the way we conventionally understand the world: the real and the unreal, the actual and the imaginary, the physical and the spiritual. This makes it difficult to read and understand, but, as has been said of Joyce's *Finnegans Wake*, when one stops trying to understand it one begins to enjoy it" (MacKenzie 154).

a temptation here, even love of what is highest and most rightly lovable" (29). How does Fernie explain himself? "I am not a rapist (not a sentence normally called for in a critical essay)," he writes, "But *Measure for Measure* troubles this admittedly minimal and unimpressive moral assertion. My life is ordinary and law-abiding but Shakespeare seems to link it to Angelo's extreme experience, discovering under also my cloak of relative decency and decorum a gross and criminal guilt. We are less equipped than was Shakespeare's day to recognize the general resonance of Angelo's weirdness" (34). I agree, because we do not, I suspect, have the moral education and vocabulary to discuss it, thus Fernie's lament about the need for some sort of theology in literature. Fernie concludes, "[I]t's Shakespeare's intimate portrayal of Angelo's tragedy of desire which has the power to get under my skin and disturb my moral self-conceit," and then, most frighteningly, "It's Angelo whom I *recognize*" (35).

This knowledge, this familiarity, is also part of Bessie Head's art. I recognize myself in Gilbert Balfour's desire to do good, in Dikeledi's tendency to take care of others, in Margaret Senior's drive to help others and prove her ideas, and in Margaret Junior's fear—all four of them—and in Elizabeth's longing for solitude, in Birgette's anxiety, and in the evil Camilla's racism and eventual racial awareness. I read Bessie Head because she addresses my own yearning for a better self by showing me, too, my lesser selves. My desire for something greater than myself, even a self greater than myself, cannot be fulfilled because of the nature of irreconcilability and because of the nature of my own personality, flawed as it is, which makes me always strive to reconcile and thus to strive against what I most want. I am too impatient and, often, too narrow-minded.

When I went home to the United States a couple of years ago to take care of some business there, I went out for a beer with my father, a Democrat, and my brother, a Republican. The conversation turned, inevitably it seemed, to politics, and I could see my father's brow furrowing, and my brother becoming flushed, and I dreaded what I thought must follow. But we got onto the nature of good and evil in human beings—this being the core of my brother's impatience with all politicians, both Republicans and Democrats. All people, he said, have a streak of evil in them, and this causes them to make bad decisions. And then I found myself carrying on a conversation about Bessie Head's ideas (even though her name never came up) with a brother with whom I had assumed that I had too little in common to ever carry on such a conversation. This event started to bring many things "home" to me in how I think about others. I started finding Bessie everywhere, even when she was not named.

And so like the spider who sheds her skin, I must now rest and reacquaint myself with myself, and begin to prepare for the next changes. Reading Bessie Head in Africa, in Botswana, has made me impatient with much Western criticism of her, because so much of it ignores this very context. Peter Carlton wrote of his own shame in abandoning his self in his efforts "to *master* and *control* the literary text" (240). That form of self-abandonment seems more and more immoral to me. By practicing this type of distancing criticism, so that I can master the text, I sense that I am losing sight of the importance of *where* exactly I am working. For African academics, and those of us non-Africans who live and work here, location is important, for we work in some ways according to a different ethic.

Working in Africa has also made me more aware of the destruction that is wrought by applying Western standards to such radically different societies. In one case, standards for Western academic processes and principles were applied wholesale to suggestions for revamping the University of Botswana (UB), with an eye to weaning academics from their families. Many people at UB pointed out that such issues regarding responsibility to others, especially family, are the foundation of Botswana's identity, and that to change how Batswana academics should work and to try to separate them from this identity would be to attack the very core of what makes people Batswana, and more generally, Africans. It will be impossible to get beyond the things that divide us if we are all asked to be just like everyone else.

Bessie Head recognizes something special in Africa, and I think she is right: a tendency to both great kindness and great cruelty, and that contradiction currently defines how much of life is lived here. I changed during my dissertation, to recognize that I am neither atheist nor Marxist, because reading Head's trilogy showed me the dangers of adhering too closely to any one set of beliefs. And I am changing now: I realize more and new things about myself that I had been resisting. I am no longer purely American, but I will never be an African since I am not entirely at home here or there, but

I am comfortable in my life wherever it is. Love is hard but necessary because taking care of people is possibly the most important thing I will ever do, even though I am selfish and resist it.

Bessie Head imagines a universal brotherhood in which all people live happy, fulfilled lives in perfect love. The necessity and impossibility of this utopia create, at least in me, the desire, the yearning for it, so that I will always come back to her having made progress and mistakes, and looking to find something else both in her and in myself.

This yearning is also its own pleasure. Fernie concludes "Mea Culpa" by intimating what is available in Shakespeare:

> I too have experienced something thing like this, a precious intimation of enlightenment which can only be accessed but is also betrayed by and remains beyond desire. But I am hardly so identified with this as Angelo is. It is through him that I acquire a better sense of it and begin to intuit what a life might be that was lived in accordance with such knowledge. In respect of Shakespeare criticism, it would mean recognizing that Shakespeare is unavailable except via a limited and partial experience which, as it were, negatively reveals what truly transcends it.
>
> But that's just Shakespeare criticism. *Measure for Measure* is about more serious things. (38)

So it is with Bessie.

# Bibliography

Abrahams, Cecil, ed. *The Tragic Life: Bessie Head and Literature in Southern Africa.* Trenton, NJ: Africa World Press, 1990.

Achebe, Chinua. "The Novelist as Teacher." *African Literature: An Anthology of Criticism and Theory.* Ed. Tejumola Olaniyan and Ato Quayson. Oxford: Blackwell, 2007. 103–6.

Altieri, Charles. "What Is at Stake in Confessional Criticism." Veeser 55–67.

Andrews, William L. "Junctions on the Color Line." Veeser 241–55.

Bazin, Nancy Topping. "Venturing into Feminist Consciousness: Bessie Head and Buchi Emecheta." Abrahams 45–58.

Bazin, Nancy Topping. "Weight of Custom, Signs of Change: Feminism in the Literature of African Women." *World Literature Written in English* 25.2 (1985): 183–97.

Beard, Linda-Susan. "Bessie Head's *A Question of Power*: The Journey Through Disintegration to Wholeness." *Colby Literary Quarterly* 15.4 (1979): 267–74.

Beard, Linda-Susan. "Bessie Head's Syncretic Fictions: The Reconceptualization of Power and the Recovery of the Ordinary." *Modern Fiction Studies* 37.3 (1991): 575–89.

Beard, Linda-Susan. "Letter by Letter: Bessie Head's Epistolary Art." Lederer, Tumedi, Molema, and Daymond 183–203.

Benedict, Ruth. *Patterns of Culture.* 1934. Boston: Houghton Mifflin, 1989.

Bennett, Bruce S. "Ecumenical Readings of Bessie Head." Lederer, Tumedi, Molema, and Daymond 72–84.

Berger, Roger. "The Politics of Madness in Bessie Head's *A Question of Power*." Abrahams 31–43.

Blakely, Mary Kay. "Psyched Out." *Los Angeles Times Magazine* 3 Oct. 1993: 27+.

Blume, Harvey. Interview. "Stephen Greenblatt: The Wicked Son." *Bookwire* June 2001. 7 Dec. 2007 <http://www.bookwire.com/bookwire/bbr/reviews/june2001/GREENBLATTInterview.htm>.

Brennan, Tim. "White-Boy Authenticity." Veeser 177–84.

Brown, Gillian. "Critical Personifications." Veeser 103–9.

Brownstein, Rachel M. "Interrupted Reading: Personal Criticism in the Present Time." Veeser 3–16.

Bruner, Charlotte. "Bessie Head: Restless in a Distant Land." *When the Drumbeat Changes*. Ed. Carolyn A. Parker and Stephen H. Arnold. Washington, DC: Three Continents Press, 1981. 261–77.

Bryce-Okunlola, Jane. "Motherhood as a Metaphor for Creativity in Three African Women's Novels: Flora Nwapa, Rebeka Njau and Bessie Head." Nasta 200–18.

Campbell, June M. "Beyond Duality: A Buddhist Reading of Bessie Head's *A Question of Power*." *Journal of Commonwealth Literature* 29.1 (1993): 64–81. *Sage*. Web. 3 March 2009.

Carlton, Peter. "Rereading *Middlemarch*, Rereading Myself." Freedman, Frey, and Zauhar 237–44.

Cary, Norman R. "Religious Discourse in the Writing of Bessie Head: A Bakhtinian Reading." *World Literature Written in English* 34.2 (1995): 38–50.

Christian, Barbara. "The Race for Theory." *Gender and Theory*. Ed. Linda Kauffmann. Oxford: Blackwell, 1989. 225–36.

Culler, Jonathan. *Literary Theory: A Very Short Introduction*. Oxford: OUP, 1997.

Darlington, Sonja. "The Significance of Bessie Head's Response to 'The Call of the Global Green.'" Lederer, Tumedi, Molema, and Daymond 46–58.

Davison, Carol Margaret. "A Method in the Madness: Bessie Head's *A Question of Power*." Abrahams 19–29.

Driver, Dorothy. "Gestures of Expatriation and Belonging." *Southern African Review of Books* Sept.–Oct. 1993: 16–18.

Eilersen, Gillian Stead. *Bessie Head: Thunder behind Her Ears. Her Life and Writing*. 1995. Johannesburg: Wits UP, 2007.

Etter-Lewis, Gwendolyn. "'Raising Hell': The Body as Text in Selected Letters of Bessie Head." Lederer, Tumedi, Molema, and Daymond 122–33.

Evasdaughter, Elizabeth N. "Bessie Head's *A Question of Power* Read as a Mariner's Guide to Paranoia." *Research in African Literatures* 20.1 (1989): 72–83.

Fanon, Frantz. *Black Skin, White Masks*. 1952. Trans. Charles Lam Markman. New York: Grove Weidenfeld, 1967.

Fernie, Ewan. "Mea Culpa." McKenzie and Papadopoulou 19–39.

Foucault, Michel. *Madness and Civilization: A History of Insanity in the Age of Reason*. 1965. Trans. Richard Howard. New York: Vintage-Random House, 1988.

Fradkin, Betty. "Conversations with Bessie." *World Literature Written in English* 17 (1978): 427–34.

Frank, Anne. *Diary of a Young Girl*. 1952. Trans. B. M. Mooyaart-Doubleday. Garden City, NY: Doubleday, 1967.

Freedman, Diane P., Olivia Frey, and Frances Murphy Zauhar, eds. *The Intimate Critique: Autobiographical Literary Criticism*. Durham, NC, and London: Duke UP, 1993.

Frey, Olivia. "Beyond Literary Darwinism: Women's Voices and Critical Discourse." Freedman, Frey, and Zauhar 41–65.

Gagiano, Annie. "Writing a Life in Epistolic Form: Bessie Head's Letters." *Journal of Literary Studies/Tydskrif vir Literatuurwetenskap* 25.1 (2009): 8–31.

Gikandi, Simon. "African Literature and the Colonial Factor." *Cambridge History of African and Caribbean Literature*, vol. 1. Ed. Abiola Irele and Simon Gikandi. Cambridge: CUP, 2004. 379–85.

Gilbert, Sandra, and Susan Gubar. *The Madwoman in the Attic: The Woman Writer and the Nineteenth-Century Literary Imagination*. New Haven, CT: Yale UP, 1979.

Gilman, Charlotte Perkins. *The Yellow Wallpaper*. 1892. Various editions.

Goodhead, Dokubo Melford. "The Discourse of Sustainable Farming and the Environment in Bessie Head's *When Rain Clouds Gather*." *Legon Journal of the Humanities* 28.1 (2017): 30–45. Doi https://dx.doi.org/10.4314/ljh.v28i1.4.

*The Gospel of Sri Ramakrishna*. 1942. Trans. Swami Nikhilānanda. Chennai, India: Sri Ramakrishna Math, 2006. 12 Dec. 2012 <http://www.belurmath.org/gospel/>.

Head, Bessie. "Africa." *The Cardinals* 141–44.

Head, Bessie. "African Religions." 1969. *A Woman Alone* 50–53.

Head, Bessie. *A Bewitched Crossroad*. Craighall, South Africa: AD. Donker, 1984.

Head, Bessie. *The Cardinals. With Meditations and Stories*. Ed. M. J. Daymond. Cape Town: David Philip, 1993.

Head, Bessie. *The Collector of Treasures and Other Botswana Village Tales*. London: Heinemann, 1977.

Head, Bessie. "The Collector of Treasures." *The Collector of Treasures and Other Botswana Village Tales* 87–102.

Head, Bessie. "Despite Broken Bondage, Botswana Women Are Still Unloved." 1975. *A Woman Alone* 54–57.

Head, Bessie. "Earth and Everything." *The Cardinals* 139–40.

Head, Bessie. *A Gesture of Belonging: Letters from Bessie Head, 1965–1979*. Ed. Randolph Vigne. Portsmouth, NH: Heinemann, 1991.

Head, Bessie. "God and the Underdog: Thoughts on the Rise of Africa." 1968. *A Woman Alone* 43–50.

Head, Bessie. "Heaven Is Not Closed." *The Collector of Treasures and Other Botswana Village Tales* 7–12.

Head, Bessie. *Imaginative Trespasser: Letters between Bessie Head, Patrick and Wendy Cullinan 1963–1977.* Ed. Patrick Cullinan. Johannesburg: Wits UP, 2005.

Head, Bessie. "My Home." *The Cardinals* 145.

Head, Bessie. "Notes from a Quiet Backwater I." 1982. *A Woman Alone* 3–5.

Head, Bessie. "Notes from a Quiet Backwater II." 1982. *A Woman Alone* 77–79.

Head, Bessie. Preface. "Witchcraft." *Ms.* 4 (1975): 72–73.

Head, Bessie. *A Question of Power.* London: Heinemann, 1974.

Head, Bessie. *Serowe: Village of the Rain Wind.* 1981. Oxford: Heinemann, 1988.

Head, Bessie. "Social and Political Pressures that Shape Writing in Southern Africa." 1979. *A Woman Alone* 65–72.

Head, Bessie. "Societal Values and Women: Images vs. Real Life." 1982/83. *English in Africa* 28.1 (2001): 47–51.

Head, Bessie. "Some Notes on Novel Writing." 1978. *A Woman Alone* 61–64.

Head, Bessie. "What Does the Botswana Novel Say?" 1981. *English in Africa* 28.1 (2001): 40–42.

Head, Bessie. *When Rain Clouds Gather and Maru.* 1969, 1971. London: Virago, 2010.

Head, Bessie. "Where Is the Hour of the Beautiful Dancing of Birds in the Sun-Wind?" *The Cardinals* 150–59.

Head, Bessie. "Why Do I Write?" 1985. *English in Africa* 28.1 (2001): 57–59.

Head, Bessie. *A Woman Alone: Autobiographical Writings.* Ed. Craig MacKenzie. Oxford: Heinemann, 1990.

Head, Bessie, and Langston Hughes. "The Bessie Head—Langston Hughes Correspondence, 1960–61." Ed. and intro. David Chioni Moore. *Research in African Literatures* 41.3 (2010): 1–20.

Highfield, Jonathan. "Relations with Food: Agriculture, Colonialism, and Foodways in the Writing of Bessie Head." *Postcolonial Green: Environmental Politics and World Narratives.* Ed. Bonnie Roos and Alex Hunt. Charlottesville and London: U of Virginia P, 2010. 102–17.

Hogan, Patrick Colm. "Bessie Head's *A Question of Power*: A Lacanian Psychosis." *Mosaic* 27.2 (1994): 95–112.

*The Holy Bible.* 1978. Cape Town: Bible Society of South Africa, 1997. Eng. New International Version.

Holzinger, Tom. "The Black Antecedents of Bessie Amelia Emery Head." Lederer, Tumedi, Molema, and Daymond 119–21.

Holzinger, Tom. "Conversations and Consternations with B Head." Lederer and Tumedi 35–57.

Holzinger, Tom. Personal correspondence. 21 Oct. 2012.

Kane, Cheikh Hamidou. *Ambiguous Adventure*. 1962. Trans. Katherine Woods. Oxford: Heinemann, 1963.

Kapstein, Helen. "'A Peculiar Shuttling Movement': Madness, Passing, and Trespassing in Bessie Head's *A Question of Power*." *Critical Essays on Bessie Head.* Ed. Maxine Sample. Westport, CT and London: Praeger, 2003. 71–98.

Kealotswe, Obed. "The Life and Prophecy in the African Independent Churches as Reflected by Bessie Head." Lederer and Tumedi 80–86.

Kerr, David. "Character, Role, Madness, God, Biography, Narrative: Dismantling and Reassembling Bessie Head's *A Question of Power*." Lederer and Tumedi 162–74.

Kiema, Kuela. *Tears for My Land: A Social History of the Kua of the Central Kalahari Game Reserve, Tc'amnqoo.* Gaborone, Botswana: Mmegi, 2010.

Kim, Sue J. "'The Real White Man is Waiting for Me': Ideology and Morality in Bessie Head's *A Question of Power*." *College Literature* 35.2 (2008): 38–69.

Laing, R. D. *The Divided Self.* 1960. Harmondsworth: Penguin, 1965.

Laing, R. D. *The Politics of Experience.* New York: Pantheon, 1967.

Laing, R. D. *Self and Others.* 1961. London: Penguin, 1990.

Lang, Candace. "Autocritique." Veeser 40–54.

Larson, Charles. *The Novel in the Third World.* Washington, DC: INSCAPE, 1976.

Lederer, Mary S. *Novels of Botswana in English, 1930–2006.* New York and Lagos: African Heritage Press, 2014.

Lederer, Mary S., and Seatholo M. Tumedi, eds. *Writing Bessie Head in Botswana: An Anthology of Remembrance and Criticism.* Gaborone, Botswana: Pentagon, 2007.

Lederer, Mary S., Seatholo M. Tumedi, Leloba S. Molema, and M. J. Daymond, eds. *The Life and Work of Bessie Head: A Celebration of the Seventieth Anniversary of Her Birth.* Gaborone, Botswana: Pentagon, 2008.

Lessing, Doris. *The Grass Is Singing.* 1950. Ontario: Plume-New American Library, 1978.

Lewis, Desiree. "Bessie Head's Freedoms." *Chimurenga Online.* Chimurenga, n.d. Web. 8 May 2010.

Lewis, Desiree. *Living on a Horizon: Bessie Head and the Politics of Imagining.* Trenton, NJ, and Asmara, Eritrea: Africa World Press, 2007.

Lorenz, Paul H. "Colonization and the Feminine in Bessie Head's *A Question of Power*." *Modern Fiction Studies* 37.3 (1991): 591–605.

MacKenzie, Craig. "A Question of Madness: Re-Reading Bessie Head's *A Question of Power*." *Current Writing* 26.2 (2014): 148–56.

Mandow, Sarah. "Boundaries and Beyond: Issues of Resistance and Control in the Work of Bessie Head." Lederer, Tumedi, Molema, and Daymond 147–60.

Maqagi, Sisi. "Epistolary Transgressions." Lederer, Tumedi, Molema, and Daymond 269–86.

Margree, Victoria. "Wild Flowers: Bessie Head on Life, Health and Botany." *Paragraph: A Journal of Modern Theory* 27.3 (2004): 16–31.

Marks, Shula, ed. *Not Either an Experimental Doll: The Separate World of Three South African Women.* Bloomington and Indianapolis: Indiana UP, 1987.

Marquard, Jean. "Bessie Head: Exile and Community in Southern Africa." *London Magazine* 18.9–10 (1988–89): 48–61.

Marquard, Jean. "The Farm: A Concept in the Writing of Olive Schreiner, Pauline Smith, Doris Lessing, Nadine Gordimer and Bessie Head." *Dalhousie Review* 59.2 (1979): 293–307.

Matsikidze, Isabella P. "Toward a Redemptive Political Philosophy: Bessie Head's *Maru.*" *World Literature Written in English* 30.2 (1990): 105–9.

Mbiti, John S. *African Religions and Philosophy.* 1969. Portsmouth, NH: Heinemann, 1990.

McBride, James. *The Color of Water: A Black Man's Tribute to His White Mother.* London: Bloomsbury, 1998.

McKenzie, William, and Theodora Papadopoulou, eds. Introduction. *Shakespeare and I* 1–18.

McKenzie, William, and Theodora Papadopoulou, eds. *Shakespeare and I.* London and New York: Continuum, 2012.

Messer-Davidow, Ellen. "The Philosophical Bases of Feminist Literary Criticisms." *New Literary History* 19.1 (1987): 65–103.

Miller-Bagley, Marilyn. "Miscegenation, Marginalization, and the Messianic in Bessie Head's *Maru.*" *World Literature Written in English* 34.2 (1995): 51–60.

Mnthali, Felix. "God and the African Novel." *Marang: A Journal of the Department of English at the University of Botswana* 11 (1995): 1–15.

Molema, Leloba S. "The Politics of Naming in *When Rain Clouds Gather.*" Lederer, Tumedi, Molema, and Daymond 22–36.

Montaigne, Michel de. *The Complete Essays.* Trans. M. A. Screech. London: Penguin, 2003.

Mosieleng, Percy. "The Condition of Exile and the Negation of Commitment: A Biographical Study of Bessie Head's Novels." *Emerging Perspectives on Bessie Head.* Ed. Huma Ibrahim. Trenton, NJ, and Asmara, Eritrea: Africa World Press, 2004. 51–71.

Nasta, Susheila. *Motherlands: Black Women's Writing from Africa, the Caribbean and South Asia.* 1991. New Brunswick, NJ: Rutgers UP, 1992.

Nkosi, Lewis. "Southern Africa: Protest and Commitment." *Tasks and Masks: Themes and Styles of African Literature*. Essex: Longman, 1981. 76–106.

Ogungbesan, Kolawole. "The Cape Gooseberry also Grows in Botswana: Alienation and Commitment in the Writings of Bessie Head." *Journal of African Studies* 6.4 (1979–80): 206–12.

Ojo-Ade, Femi. "Bessie Head's Alienated Heroine: Victim or Villain?" *Ba Shiru* 8.2 (1977): 13–21.

Ola, Virginia. "Power and the Question of Good and Evil in Bessie Head's Novels." Abrahams 59–72.

Olaogun, Modupe O. "Irony and Schizophrenia in Bessie Head's *Maru*." *Research in African Literatures* 25.4 (1994): 69–87.

Olaussen, Maria. *Forceful Creation in Harsh Terrain: Place and Identity in Three Novels by Bessie Head*. Frankfurt am Main: Peter Lang, 1997.

Pearse, Adetokunbo. "Apartheid and Madness: Bessie Head's *A Question of Power*." *Kunapipi* 5.2 (1983): 81–98.

Philip, Mark. "Michel Foucault." *The Return of Grand Theory in the Human Sciences*. Ed. Quentin Skinner. Cambridge: CUP, 1995. 65–81.

Pucherova, Dobrota. "A Romance That Failed: Bessie Head and Black Nationalism in 1960s South Africa." *Research in African Literatures* 42.2 (2011): 105–24.

Ravenscroft, Arthur. "The Novels of Bessie Head." *Aspects of South African Literature*. Ed. Christopher Heywood. New York: Africana, 1976. 174–86.

Rhodes, Jewell Parker. *Voodoo Dreams: A Novel of Marie Laveau*. New York: Picador, 1993.

Robinson, Marilynne. "Reclaiming a Sense of the Sacred." *The Chronicle of Higher Education*. 12 Feb. 2012. Web. 13 Feb. 2012.

Rooney, Caroline. "'Dangerous Knowledge' and the Poetics of Survival: A Reading of *Our Sister Killjoy* and *A Question of Power*." Nasta 99–126.

Rose, Jacqueline. "On the 'Universality' of Madness: Bessie Head's *A Question of Power*." *Critical Inquiry* 20 (1994): 401–18.

Rowling, J. K. *Harry Potter and the Deathly Hallows*. London: Bloomsbury, 2007.

Roy, Modhumita. "'Everyone Had a Place in My World': Bessie Head's Utopia in *When Rain Clouds Gather*." Lederer, Tumedi, Molema, and Daymond 255–68.

Sample, Maxine. "Landscape and Spatial Metaphor in Bessie Head's *The Collector of Treasures*." *Studies in Short Fiction* 28.3 (1991): 311–19.

Setiloane, Gabriel M. *The Image of God Among the Sotho-Tswana*. Rotterdam: A. A. Balkema, 1976.

Shaw, George Bernard. *Maxims for Revolutionists*. 1903. 10 Nov. 2017 http://www.panarchy.org/shaw/maxims.1903.html.

Siletshena, R. M. K. "Migration and Permanent Settlement at the Lands Area." *Proceedings of the Symposium on Settlement in Botswana—The Historical Development of a Human Landscape. National Museum, Gaborone, Botswana, August 4th to 8th, 1980.* Ed. R. Renée Hitchcock and Mary R. Smith. Gaborone, Botswana: Heinemann and The Botswana Society, 1982. 220–31.

Slaymaker, William. "Echoing the Other(s): The Call of the Global Green and Black African Responses." *PMLA* 116.1 (2001): 129–44.

Smith, Lauren. "Christ as Creole: Hybridity and the Revision of Colonial Imagery in the Works of Bessie Head." *English in Africa* 26.1 (1999): 61–80.

Talahite, Anissa. "Cape Gooseberries and Giant Cauliflowers: Transplantation, Hybridity, and Growth in Bessie Head's *A Question of Power.*" *Mosaic: A Journal for the Interdisciplinary Study of Literature* 38.4 (2005): 141–56.

Tompkins, Jane. "Me and My Shadow." Freedman, Frey, and Zauhar 23–40.

Tucker, Margaret E. "A 'Nice-Time Girl' Strikes Back: An Essay on Bessie Head's *A Question of Power.*" *Research in African Literatures* 19.2 (1988): 170–81.

Tulloch, Elspeth. "Husbandry, Agriculture and Ecocide: Reading Bessie Head's *When Rain Clouds Gather* as a Postcolonial Georgic." *European Journal of English Studies* 16.2 (2012): 137–50. DOI 10.1080/13825577.2012.70389.

U2. "I Still Haven't Found What I'm Looking for." Lyrics by Bono. *The Joshua Tree.* Island Records, 1987. CD.

Vanamali, Rukmini. "Bessie Head's *A Question of Power*: The Mythic Dimension." *The Literary Criterion* 23.1–2 (1988): 154–71.

Veeser, H. Aram, ed. *Confessions of the Critics.* New York and London: Routledge, 1996.

Vigne, Randolph. "Introduction." *A Gesture of Belonging* 1–8.

Walker, Alice. *The Color Purple.* New York: Harcourt, Brace, Jovanovich, 1982.

Wilhelm, Cherry. "Bessie Head: The Face of Africa." *English in Africa* 10.1 (1983): 1–13.

Zauhar, Frances Murphy. "Creative Voices: Women Reading and Women's Writing." Freedman, Frey, and Zauhar 103–16.

Zinato, Susanna. "Introduction: Treating Madness with Style." *The House Is Empty: Grammars of Madness in J. Frame's* Scented Gardens for the Blind *and B. Head's* A Question of Power. Bologna: CLUEB, 1999. 16–44.

# Index

San 89, 91
  terminology 59
sanity, as social interaction 78
*Das Schloß* (Franz Kafka) 29
Setiloane, Gabriel 117n. 13
*Shakespeare and I* (McKenzie and
    Papadopoulou) 136, 140–2, 144
Shaw, George Bernard 44n. 14
Swami Vivekananda 109

*Tears for My Land* (Kuela Kiema) 59n. 10

Vanamali, Rukmini 104n. 3, 105n. 4, 131
Vigne, Randolph 1, 60n. 13, 76, 103
  Dorothy Driver's review of letters 103–4,
    117
  Bessie Head's ideas on God as man 112,
    113, 119
  Bessie Head's interview with Miriam
    Makeba 93n. 15

Walker, Alice 49–50, 80
  *The Color Purple* 112
"*Weltgeheimnis*" (Hugo von Hoffmansthal)
    10
*When Rain Clouds Gather* 54–8
  Bessie Head's critique of 57
  complementarity in 98–9
  God (Good God) 121–3
  good and evil in 121
  love and responsibility 57–8
  men and women in 88
  whiteness 137–8
Wicomb, Zoë 1
"Winds of Change" (lost novel) 8n. 15
"*Das Wort*" (Stefan George) 10
work 54–6, 95
  and community 78
  and responsibility for others 56, 57